REVELATION

CHARLES CALDWELL RYRIE

REVELATION

MOODY PRESS • CHICAGO

ISBN: 0-8024-2066-4

Seventeenth Printing, 1979

CONTENTS

CHAPTER   PAGE

	Introduction	7
I	The Prologue, 1:1-8	13
II	The Vision of Christ, 1:9-20	16
III	The Seven Churches, 2:1—3:22	20
IV	The Throne in Heaven, 4:1-11	33
V	The Seven-Sealed Book, 5:1-14	39
VI	The Six Seals, 6:1-17	43
VII	The Redeemed of the Tribulation, 7:1-17	49
VIII	The First Four Trumpets, 8:1-13	55
IX	Woes on the Earth, 9:1-21	60
X	The Angel and the Little Opened Book, 10:1-11	66
XI	The Temple, the Two Witnesses and the Trumpet, 11:1-19	71
XII	War, 12:1-17	77
XIII	The Beast and His Prophet, 13:1-18	82
XIV	Various Announcements, 14:1-20	88
XV	Prelude to the Last Judgments, 15:1-8	94

XVI   The Seven Bowl Judgments, 16:1-21   96

XVII   Religious Babylon, 17:1-18   100

XVIII   Commercial Babylon, 18:1-24   105

XIX   The Second Coming of Christ, 19:1-21   110

XX   The Millennium and the Great White
        Throne, 20:1-15   114

XXI   The Eternal State, 21:1—22:5   118

XXII   Epilogue, 22:6-21   124

        Some Helpful Commentaries on Revelation   127

INTRODUCTION

EACH BOOK of the Bible is important, but the last book is the consummation and climax of God's revelation.

Revelation is primarily significant because it is a book about "things which must shortly come to pass." Many of these things we would not know if the book of Revelation were not in the Bible. It is the only major prophetic book in the New Testament.

John was commanded not to seal the book (22:10), and those who read it are promised a special blessing (1:3). Apparently, therefore, the book was expected to be intelligible and helpful to those who read it. It is an apocalypse (literally, a revelation), designed not to mystify, but to clarify.

AUTHOR AND DATE

According to the book itself, the author's name was John (1:4, 9; 22:8), who was a prophet (22:9). He was a leader in the churches of Asia Minor (chaps. 2–3), and was one of the earliest disciples of the Lord. His family were fishermen, and apparently prosperous (Matt. 4:21). He, along with James and Peter, bore a unique relationship to the Lord (Mark 5: 37; 13:3). John is mentioned only three times in the book of Acts (3:1; 4:13; 8:14), and tradition says that he settled in Ephesus, where he was later arrested and banished under the Emperor Domitian to Patmos (a small island in the Aegean

Sea) to work in the mines.* Domitian reigned from A.D. 81-96,
and since Irenaeus' testimony that John wrote Revelation
while on Patmos is confirmed by other early writers, the book
is believed to be one of the last written of the New Testament.
This late date is also confirmed by the picture of complacency
and defection in the churches in chapters 2 and 3. This fact
presupposes that there had come on the scene a second genera-
tion of Christians who did not hold the same convictions as
their fathers.

INTERPRETATION

The book is a revelation of things which must shortly come
to pass. The understanding of when the events of the book
will come to pass marks the difference between the various
schools of interpretation.

PRETERIST

"Preterist" is from a Latin word which means "past." Thus
the preterist interpreters are those who see Revelation as having already been fulfilled in the early history of the church.
Chapters 5—11 are said to record the church's victory over
Judaism; chapters 12—19, her victory over pagan Rome; and
20—22 her glory because of these victories. The persecutions
described are those of Nero and Domitian, and the entire
book was fulfilled by the time of Constantine (A.D. 312).

HISTORICAL OR CONTINUOUS-HISTORICAL

This interpretative viewpoint states that in Revelation there
is a panorama of the history of the church from the days of
John to the end of the age. It holds that the book has been
in the process of being fulfilled throughout the whole Christian
era. Those who hold this view see in the symbols the rise of
the papacy, the corruption of the church and the various wars

*Saint Irenaeus, *Libros Quinque Adversus Haereses* (Against Her-
esies), V, XXX, 3.

throughout church history. Most of the Reformers interpreted the book in this manner, but every man's interpretation within this viewpoint is a scheme all its own. There is no uniformity of details; indeed, there is much dogmatism and contradiction among those who attempt to interpret the book this way.

IDEALIST

This approach sees in Revelation a pictorial unfolding of great principles in constant conflict. The book does not record actual events which have been fulfilled or which are going to come to pass; rather, it merely portrays the agelong struggle between good and evil. This viewpoint spiritualizes and allegorizes the text.

FUTURIST OR PLAIN INTERPRETATION

The label "futurist" is derived from the fact that this interpretation sees the book from chapter 4 on as yet to be fulfilled. If one follows the plain, literal or normal principle of interpretation he concludes that most of the book is yet in the future. No judgments in history have ever equaled those described in chapters 6, 8, 9 and 16. The resurrections and judgment described in chapter 20 have not yet occurred. There has been no visible return of Christ as portrayed in chapter 19.

The concept of a literal interpretation always raises questions since it seems to preclude anything symbolic, and the book obviously contains symbols. Perhaps saying "normal" or "plain" interpretation would be better than "literal," since futurists do recognize the presence of symbols in the book. The difference between the literalist and the spiritualizer is simply that the former sees the symbols as conveying a plain meaning. All recognize the presence of symbols in the Bible. Note, for instance, Psalm 22. Verse 18 prophesied the casting of lots for Christ's garments. This was a literal statement. Verses 12 and 13 depict the fierce enemies of the Lord as strong bulls and ravening lions. These are symbols with a very plain meaning.

Revelation 8:12 prophesies a judgment which will affect the sun, moon, stars, day and night. Apparently the stars are literally the astronomical bodies in the heavens. In 9:1-2 John records seeing a star fall from heaven. This is a plain symbol and one that is interpreted in the text itself as indicating a created being (probably an angel). The English word "star" is used today in both a literal and symbolic manner just as it is in Revelation 8 and 9. We speak literally of the stars in the heavens. We also refer to stars on the athletic field and in so doing we are using a symbol with a very plain meaning. Indeed, symbols often make the meaning more plain. The futurist does not deny the presence of symbols in the book, nor does he claim to be able to explain every detail with certainty. But he does insist that the principle of plain interpretation be followed consistently throughout the book.

ATTITUDES

Generally speaking there are two extreme attitudes toward Revelation. Some say the book cannot be understood, and therefore it should be not studied, taught or preached. Differences of interpretation, they point out, have divided Christians, and therefore the book should not be interpreted. Others consider themselves so sure of every detail of the book that they set dates and propose highly fanciful interpretations. To them Revelation seems to be the only book in the Bible worth studying.

The proper attitude toward this book does not lie in either extreme. The book is important and profitable as is all Scripture (II Tim. 3:16), but it is not the only book in the Bible. Let us approach it as worthy of all the Spirit-directed study we can give it, focusing every God-given ability on its words, and fitting it into the whole of God's truth as given in the Bible. Let our approach never be theoretical and detached but always personal and involved. Even though this book is largely about the future, knowledge of it should affect our living in the present. James encouraged his contemporaries with the knowledge of future judgment (James 5:8), and Paul told of the assurance that Satan would eventually be defeated (Rom. 16:20). And God can motivate believers today by the understanding of those things which He has revealed through John in Revelation.

I

THE PROLOGUE

1:1-8

TITLE, 1:1

WHILE IT IS TRUE that this book reveals Christ, the genitive "of Jesus Christ" means that it is *a* revelation given by Christ. It is a revelation of "things which must shortly come to pass." The words translated "shortly" (*en tachei*) mean that when the time of vengeance comes there will be no delay in its execution. (See Luke 18:8 and other occurrences in Acts 12:7; 22:18; 25:4; Rom. 16:20 and Rev. 22:6-7.) The time of the fulfillment may seem distant but when it does come the events will transpire with rapidity.

COMMUNICATION, 1:1-2

The chain of communication was: God the Father, to Christ, to an angel, to John, to God's servants. John, the human instrument, testified of the Word of God (he considered himself in the prophetic succession, transmitting God's message to man) and the testimony of Christ, that is, the witness which Christ imparts about Himself.

13

VALUE, 1:3

A blessing is promised the one reading and those hearing and keeping the words of the book. Note the change from singular to plural—one reads and several hear—indicating that the book was read publicly. This public reading was a test of canonicity, so that the fact that John indicates it should be read publicly means that he considered it canonical. The entire book is called a prophecy. The phrase "the time is at hand" is repeated in the epilogue (22:10). "At hand" (*eggus*) means proximity or nearness, and these events are at hand since a thousand years are as a day with the Lord.

SALUTATION, 1:4-8

WRITER, 1:4

The Hebrew idioms in the book, the authority of the author in relation to the churches, the use of distinctively Johannine terms like *logos* and "Lamb of God," and the corroboration of Irenaeus, Origen, Tertullian and Clement all affirm that the Apostle John was the author of this book.

READERS, 1:4

The fact that John specifically addressed the seven local churches in Asia Minor prevents anyone from saying that the book is simply a piece of poetic idealism.

GREETING, 1:4-5a

This is a greeting from the Trinity. The Father eternally existed and will always exist (the phrase occurs also in 1:8; 4:8; 11:17; 16:5). The "seven Spirits" likely represent the sevenfold ministry of the Spirit as depicted in Isaiah 11:2. Christ is designated as (1) the faithful Witness (summarizing His life on earth, cf. John 7:7; 8:18; I Tim. 6:13), (2) the Firstborn from the dead (His resurrection), and (3) the Ruler (not "prince") of the kings of the earth, which refers to His future rule over the earth.

DEDICATION, 1:5*b*-6

The book is dedicated to Christ who was its Author, and about whom it speaks. Three things are ascribed to Him: (1) He loves (present tense) us. (2) He loosed us (some texts read "washed," the difference in Greek being one letter) from our sins in His blood. Blood is the evidence of His death which is the basis for our cleansing. (3) He made us a kingdom (not kings) and priests to God. "Kingdom" views believers corporately and anticipates our association with Christ in His reign (5:9-10), while "priests" sees them individually.

KEYNOTE, 1:7

Verse 7 is the text, theme or keynote of the book, and is a reference to Christ's second coming. It is after the tribulation (note Matt. 24:29-30); it will be public; and all shall see Him and bemoan His crucifixion. This is partly quoted from Zechariah 12:10. "Kindreds" is not limited to Israel but includes all the peoples of the earth.

AUTHENTICATION, 1:8

Some understand the speaker in verse 8 to be God; others, Christ. It is probably God verifying the contents of this prophecy. Alpha and Omega are the first and last letters of the Greek alphabet, signifying the completeness of God. He is the Lord God, eternally existing, and all powerful. "Almighty" is used eight times in Revelation and includes the ideas of omnipotence and universal rulership.

II

THE VISION OF CHRIST
1:9-20

ALTHOUGH there are several ways to divide the book of Revelation, most commentators see in 1:19 a divinely given outline. In this verse the book is divided into three parts: (1) the things which John had seen up to verse 19, (2) the present state of the church (chaps. 2—3), and (3) the things which shall be after the church is completed (chaps. 4—22). The words translated "hereafter" (*meta tauta*) mean literally "after these things." The same words are found in 4:1, indicating that chapter 4 begins this last section of the book. However, it is possible to combine the first two sections because verse 19 may well be translated, "Write the things which thou hast seen, *both* the things which are and. . . ."

In other words, John saw two things: present things and future things. The present things include the vision of Christ in 1:9-20 and the letters to the churches in chapters 2 and 3. Of course it does make sense to see 1:9—3:22 as one unified section, simply because in the vision in 1:9-20 Christ is walking in the midst of those churches mentioned in chapters 2 and 3. But it is equally valid to consider the vision of 1:9-20 as that which John had seen and thus as a separate division of the book. The important thing is to notice that according to 1:19 the book has to divide at 4:1, regardless of whether one combines the vision of 1:9-20 with chapters 2 and 3 or divides it into a separate section.

SECTION I: "THE THINGS WHICH THOU HAST SEEN," 1:9-20

CIRCUMSTANCES OF THE VISION, 1:9-11

PHYSICAL CIRCUMSTANCES, 1:9

John does not exalt himself above his fellow believers but calls himself a brother. Patmos is an island about fifteen miles in circumference in the Aegean Sea southwest of Ephesus. The reason for his banishment was "for," literally, "because of" the Word of God (God's claims on men) and the testimony of Jesus (the gospel message).

SPIRITUAL CIRCUMSTANCES, 1:10-11

John's being in the Spirit seems to indicate a trancelike state of spiritual ecstasy. "Was" is literally "became," indicating that this was something unusual. The phrase "the Lord's day" could refer to Sunday or the day of the Lord, that is, the tribulation and the millennium which are the subject of much of the prophecy. "Lord's" is an adjective (*kuriakos*) which is used only here and in I Corinthians 11:20 in the New Testament. Outside the New Testament it means "imperial." Unless this be a reference to Sunday, there is no place in the New Testament where this expression is used for that day since the usual designation is "first day of the week." It could then refer to that imperial day in the future when Christ will take the reins of earthly government which was what John saw in his vision. The voice which John heard was that of Christ who is identified as the First and Last in verse 17. All that John saw (cf. 22:8), not just the particular letter to each church in chapters 2—3, was to be communicated to all these seven churches mentioned in verse 11.

CONTENT OF THE VISION, 1:12-16

POSITION OF THE LORD, 1:12-13

The Lord is described as "like unto the Son of man." This means that His form was humanlike. He was in the midst of seven lampstands. These are explained in verse 20 as the seven churches of verse 11. Notice that the Lord has a direct relationship to each church. His clothing (v. 13) is that of a priest and judge, which are the relationships of authority which He sustains to the local churches.

PICTURE OF THE LORD, 1:14-16

This is a picture of the risen, glorified Lord depicted under a number of similes—the only way He could be described to finite creatures (note the occurrences of "like" and "as"). There are seven features to this picture, and the meaning of these similes may have been unexplained deliberately in order to convey more than one thing to our minds.

His head, 1:14. It was white as wool or snow. This may represent the wisdom of age and the purity of holiness.

His eyes, 1:14. They were piercing in their fiery holiness. The true character of each church is transparent to His eyes. There may also be a connection between this verse and I Corinthians 3:13; that is, the fire which shall try men's works at the judgment seat of Christ will be the gaze of Christ which will of itself consume works of wood, hay and stubble.

His feet, 1:15. His feet were like burnished bronze (literal translation). This may indicate the trials He experienced in His earthly life which make Him a sympathetic High Priest (Heb. 4:15) and an experienced Judge.

His voice, 1:15. It was to John as the sound of many waters. Like the noise of a mighty waterfall His voice of authority stands out above all the rest.

His right hand, 1:16. In His right hand, the place of honor, were the seven stars which are explained in verse 20 as the messengers of the churches of chapters 2—3. The word *angel* means messenger and could mean a supernatural being, implying that each church has its guardian angel. Or the word could be used in a nontechnical sense as a human messenger (see James 2:25 and Luke 9:52) —the human leader or pastor of the church.

His mouth, 1:16. The Word of God, the basis for all judgment, proceeded out of His mouth (Heb. 4:12; Rev. 19:13-15).

His countenance, 1:16. Christ's overall appearance was such that it overwhelmed John.

CONSEQUENCES OF THE VISION, 1:17-20

A WORD OF COMFORT, 1:17-18

The awesomeness of the vision caused John to prostrate himself before the glorified Christ. This resulted in a threefold word of comfort for the aged apostle. Christ presented Himself as the self-existent, eternal One, "the first and the last"; the Conqueror over death; and the One who controls (by having the keys) Hades (the place that holds the immaterial part of man after death) and death (the condition of the material part).

A WORD OF COMMAND, 1:19-20

The apostle is then commanded to write the things which he had seen and would yet see. As stated, this forms an outline of the book, and is followed in verse 20 by the Lord's own explanation of two features of the vision.

III

THE SEVEN CHURCHES
2:1—3:22

THE SEVEN CHURCHES addressed by letter in chapters 2 and 3 are significant in several ways. First of all, at the time John wrote, they were actual churches which existed in the cities mentioned. They were apparently not the most prominent ones of that day since only two—Ephesus and Laodicea—are previously mentioned in the Bible. But they were actual churches with the problems and strengths recorded of them. This means, of course, that just as there was an Ephesian church in John's day, there was also a Laodicean church in the first century.

These churches were representative of all churches at that time as well as subsequent generations. Just as the letters to the Corinthians, though written to the church at Corinth, concern the church everywhere and at all times, so these letters are for the church past, present and future. Two reasons substantiate the representative character of these seven churches. The first is simply the fact that there are seven. Out of all the churches that might have been chosen (like Jerusalem, Antioch, Alexandria, Corinth, Rome, Colosse or Hierapolis) only these seven are selected. Second, in the promise to each of these churches at the close of each letter is the exhortation to hear what the Spirit says to "the churches." Though each letter is written to *a* church, the promise is to all the church*es*.

The third significance of these churches is more debated, but some regard the seven churches as representing the various successive periods of church history. One writer says, "The varying conditions represented in these seven churches in order of their succession fit uniquely into the checkered history of the church universal from start to finish."* This idea does not deny their local and representative character; it simply adds a prophetic significance.

Each letter is addressed to the angel of the particular church. The word *angel,* as previously discussed, can refer to either superhuman or human beings. In either case their places of responsibility cause them to share in the blessing and blame of congregations.

SECTION II: "THE THINGS WHICH ARE," 2:1—3:22

These letters comprise the "things which are." They depict conditions which did and do exist in the churches then and now. Each letter may be outlined under six headings: Destination, The Lord, Commendation, Condemnation, Exhortation and Promise.

THE MESSAGE TO EPHESUS, 2:1-7

DESTINATION, 2:1

Ephesus was the capital of the province of Asia, abode of John before and after his exile on Patmos, and the home of one of the seven wonders of the ancient world—the temple of Diana. The church in that city was established by Paul on the third missionary journey (Acts 19), and it could also count Aquila, Priscilla, Apollos, Timothy and John among its spiritual leaders. Ephesus (meaning "desirable") may represent the Apostolic Age.

*J. B. Smith, *A Revelation of Jesus Christ* (Scottdale, Pa.: Herald Press, 1961), p. 61.

THE LORD, 2:1

In each letter the risen Christ presents Himself in a particular fashion selected for the most part from the representation in chapter 1 which is especially relevant to the condition of the church addressed. In this instance (in view of the loss of first love) the Lord's watchful relationship to local churches and their leaders is emphasized in two ways: He is seen holding fast (*krateo*) the seven stars or angels (in contrast to 1:16 where He merely has them), and He is walking (in contrast to standing, 1:13) in the midst of the churches.

COMMENDATION, 2:2-3, 6

The church is commended for her works, patience (endurance), discernment in testing, rejecting false apostles and hatred of the Nicolaitans. Some understand the Nicolaitan error to be the exaltation of the clergy over the laity (based on the etymology of the word itself which means "laity-conqueror"). Others consider it to be the heresy of antinomianism or compromise, since it is associated in 2:14-15 with the doctrine of Balaam, who tried to induce God's people to compromise.

CONDEMNATION, 2:4

The church had left (not "lost") her first love. This was a responsible action, for the word means to quit or forsake. The original spiritual vitality of the church had been replaced by an orthodox routine.

EXHORTATION, 2:5-6

The exhortation was to remember, repent and repeat her first works of love.

PROMISE, 2:7

An overcomer is not someone who has some special power in the Christian life or someone who has learned some secret of victory. John himself defined an overcomer as a believer in Christ (I John 5:4-5). Thus every Christian is an overcomer, though the various promises in these seven letters are addressed particularly to each local believing group, and tailored to the special circumstances found in each church. Believers here are promised the tree of life; that is, eternal life which was lost when Adam sinned in the garden (Gen. 2:9; 3:22; Rev. 22:2, 14).

THE MESSAGE TO SMYRNA, 2:8-11

DESTINATION, 2:8

Smyrna, about thirty-five miles north of Ephesus, was and continues to be an important seaport city. It was a beautiful city and the site of a temple erected in honor of the Emperor Tiberias. There were many apostate Jews there who were often leaders in agitating persecution of Christians. The word itself means bitter, being translated elsewhere in the New Testament as myrrh (Matt. 2:11; Mark 15:23; John 19:39). As a representative church it pictures the postapostolic era up to the time when Constantine espoused the Christian faith.

THE LORD, 2:8

To a church under persecution, many of whose members would experience martyrdom, the Lord appropriately presents Himself as the One who died and lived, thus assuring them of the hope of resurrection.

COMMENDATION, 2:9

The church is commended for its wealth in the midst of the most trying circumstances. Of course this is spiritual wealth, for they were poor and persecuted. The instigators of the persecution were apostate Jews who were in reality instruments of Satan. At the martyrdom of Polycarp at Smyrna in 168, these Jews eagerly assisted by gathering *on the Sabbath* wood and fagots for the fire in which he was burned.

ENCOURAGEMENT, 2:10

In place of any word of condemnation (as also in the case of the church at Philadelphia) there is an exhortation not to fear and a promise of a crown of life for faithfulness (cf. James 1:12). Satan would move men to cast some of these believers into prison, and persecution for "ten days" would result in some being killed. The ten days may refer to a brief, intense time of trouble or it may indicate the ten principal persecutions under the Roman emperors from Nero to Diocletian.

PROMISE, 2:11

The promise to the believer-overcomer is that he shall not have a part in the second death which is the lake of fire (20: 14; 21:8). In other words, the believer will share in resurrection, not in the destruction which awaits the unbeliever. The certainty of this promise is emphasized by the use of a double negative in the text.

THE MESSAGE TO PERGAMUM, 2:12-17

DESTINATION, 2:12

The two parts of the name Pergamum (about forty-five miles north of Smyrna and seventy-five miles north of Ephesus) mean elevation and marriage. For many centuries it was an independent kingdom, but became part of the Roman Empire in 133 B.C. and the location of the only provincial temple of the imperial cult in Asia erected in honor of Augustus Caesar (who reigned when Jesus was born). It also boasted one of the finest libraries of antiquity and was the place parchment was first used. The church may picture the period beginning with the legalizing of Christianity by Constantine in A.D. 313.

THE LORD, 2:12, cf. 1:16

The two-edged sword is the symbol of the word of Christ, the asurance of judgment on the basis of absolute truth.

COMMENDATION, 2:13

The Lord commends the church for its steadfastness in the very center of Satan's domination. Antipas (either one of their members or someone brought to Pergamum for trial) had already suffered martyrdom. Satan's seat is literally Satan's throne and refers to pagan Pergamum's worship either of the Roman emperor or of the Greek gods in the temple, or of Zeus at his altar on the Acropolis (or all three).

CONDEMNATION, 2:14-15

The condemnation was in the realm of morals (doctrine of Balaam) and of doctrine (of the Nicolaitans). Balaam (Num. 22:1–25:9), finding himself unable to curse God's people, instructed Balak, king of Moab, to corrupt them through immorality and idolatry so that God eventually judged them. His doctrine is the teaching of compromise in life. The doctrine of the Nicolaitans may be the same teaching (i.e., compromise) or it may be an unwarranted exaltation of the clergy.

EXHORTATION, 2:16

The call to repentance is coupled with a warning of judgment on the basis of the Word of God.

PROMISE, 2:17

Hidden manna is the sufficiency of Christ in contrast to the allurements of the world which compromise offered. The meaning of the white stone with the new name written is derived from either or both of two customs of the day. The first was that of judges who determined a verdict by placing in an urn a white and a black pebble. If the white one came out it meant acquittal; thus the white stone would mean the assurance that there is no condemnation to those who are in Christ Jesus. The other custom was the wearing of amulets as good luck charms around the neck. If this is the reference, then the stone is the Lord's way of reminding the people that they had Him and needed no other thing.

The Message to Thyatira, 2:18-29

DESTINATION, 2:18

Thyatira, about thirty-five miles southeast of Pergamum, was noted for its numerous trade guilds and for its wool and dyeing industry. It was the home of Lydia (Acts 16:14). The name means unweary sacrifice, and if these churches picture eras of church history, Thyatira—both because of its name and the activity of Jezebel—depicts the Middle Ages and the ascendancy of the Roman church.

THE LORD, 2:18

The Lord presents Himself to this church as the divine One ("Son of God") who is the Executor of searching judgment ("eyes like unto a flame of fire").

COMMENDATION, 2:19

The church is commended for its increasing works, for the last were more than the first.

CONDEMNATION, 2:20-23

The church is rebuked for permitting the false teaching of a prophetess who openly advocated apostasy. Her actual name may or may not have been Jezebel, but she was a true Jezebel in her actions (I Kings 16; II Kings 9). She promoted immorality and idolatry (v. 20) in a doctrinal context which is described as the "depths [deep things] of Satan" (v. 24). Because she had not repented at the patience of God, He promised to judge her by allowing her a complete abandonment to her way of life (v. 22), trouble for her associates (v. 22), and eventual death resulting in a purified church (v. 23).

EXHORTATION, 2:24-25

The exhortation to those who had not trafficked with Jezebel was "none other burden" than that they should keep from immorality and idolatry. The phrase is an echo of Acts 15: 28-29.

PROMISE, 2:26-28

The faithful are promised association with Christ in His millennial reign (vv. 26-27, cf. Ps. 2:9) and "the morning star" (v. 28). This is a reference to Christ Himself (cf. 22:16) and probably an attempt to call them back to a vital loyalty to Him.

THE MESSAGE TO SARDIS, 3:1-6

DESTINATION, 3:1

Sardis, about thirty miles south of Thyatira, was the capital of Lydia. The city was thought to be impregnable, but Cyrus, king of the Medo-Persians, captured it by following a secret path up the cliff. The word Sardis is probably from a Hebrew word meaning rest or remnant. This church may represent the Reformation period.

THE LORD, 3:1

The Lord appears as the One who is full of wisdom (seven spirits) and who is in complete control of the leadership of the churches (seven stars, cf. 1:20).

COMMENDATION, 3:4

In a sense it is true to say that there is no commendation of this church but only recognition of the few faithful in Sardis. The church as a whole, however, had failed.

CONDEMNATION, 3:1-2

The church is first condemned for its lifeless profession (v. 1*b*). The One who knows all things discerned the true condition of the church as being dead, though outwardly it seemed alive. Second, the church is condemned for its incomplete works (v. 2, "perfect" should be rendered "full" or "complete").

EXHORTATION, 3:3

Like the church at Ephesus, this one is exhorted to remember what they had received and heard in the first days of their Christian experience (cf. Heb. 10:32; Gal. 5:7). The people are also exhorted to watch for the Lord's coming and be prepared (I Thess. 5:6-8).

PROMISE, 3:5-6

To the true believing element in the church is promised white raiment, a sign of purity (cf. 19:8, 14). The grace of the Lord is displayed in the statement of verse 4 that these few are worthy to walk with the Lord in purity. The certainty of the promise is assured because these will not (emphatic double negative) be blotted out of the book of life (cf. 20:12). Also, these faithful ones will be acknowledged publicly before the Father and His angels.

THE MESSAGE TO PHILADELPHIA, 3:7-13

DESTINATION, 3:7

Philadelphia, about twenty-eight miles southeast of Sardis, means brotherly love. The city was named after King Attalus III. It bordered on Mysia, Lydia and Phrygia, and because it was liable to severe earthquakes, many of its inhabitants lived outside the city limits. This church may picture the modern missionary era of church history.

THE LORD, 3:7

The Head of the church presents Himself as holy, true and authoritative. The last part of verse 7 is taken from Isaiah

22:22, where authority was given God's servant Eliakim over David's house.

COMMENDATION, 3:8

The church is commended for four things: (1) using the opportunities afforded by the open door (this seems to be implied in v. 8*a*) ; (2) a little power (not so much an indication of spiritual weakness as of the few true saints in the church) ; (3) keeping His Word; (4) separation and fidelity.

PROMISES, 3:9-11*a*, 12-13

Five promises are given.

Enemies would be humiliated. Their enemies would be humiliated before them (v. 9). As in Smyrna, these unbelieving Jewish antagonists are called the "synagogue of Satan" (2:9).

Church promised deliverance. The church is also promised deliverance from the hour of trial which shall come upon all the world. The words "temptation" or "trial" are equivalents for "tribulation" (cf. Luke 8:13 with Matt. 13:21 and Mark 4:17). The verse indicates that this does not refer to the normal trials of Christians but to a special hour of trial which will be worldwide. Even the persecutions which believers have and are suffering today at the hands of particular nations do not fulfill this verse since they are not worldwide. The promise of the Lord is that the church will be kept from that hour. It is well known that the phrase "keep from" is used only twice in the New Testament—here and in John 17:15. In the latter reference the Lord prayed that believers would be kept from the evil one, which prayer is answered by delivering us from the power of darkness, transferring us into the kingdom of His dear Son (Col. 1:13). In this passage believers are promised to be kept from that hour.

The most natural meaning of the promise includes transferring us to heaven from the earth where the hour of trial will

be going on. It is possible to conceive of the church's being
protected from the judgments of the tribulation period while
remaining on earth, but we know that God's saints on the
earth during that time will not be exempt from the judgments
or from death (6:9-11; 7:9-14; 14:1-3; 15:1-3). One might be
kept from the tribulation without a pretribulation rapture,
but how can one be kept from the hour without being raptured? If the church will not be raptured before the hour begins, then the promise will not be fulfilled because many saints
simply will not be preserved but will suffer and die.

Lord to come quickly. The Lord promises to come quickly
(v. 11).

Believers to be honored. The promise that believers will be
pillars may allude to the custom in Philadelphia of honoring
a magistrate or philanthropist by placing a great pillar in one
of the temples with his name inscribed on it. Believers will be
so honored in the temple of God and permanently so ("shall
go no more out").

Saints to have God's name. God promises to write on the
saints His name, the name of His city and His new name.
What the new name may be we do not know, but the writing
of a name indicates identification with, and possession by, God.

These must have been very precious promises to a church
that was plagued by enemies within and without, and they will
always be precious promises to the church universal.

EXHORTATION, 3:11*b*

The only exhortation is to hold fast (the same word is used
in 2:1, 13-14, 25). The reason for this exhortation is that no one
would rob them of their rewards (cf. II John 8).

THE MESSAGE TO LAODICEA, 3:14-21

DESTINATION, 3:14

These seven churches lie within a great arc beginning with

Ephesus, swinging upward and eastward through Smyrna and Pergamum and back down to Laodicea. Thus this last city is about ninety miles due east of Ephesus and about forty-five miles southeast of Philadelphia. The name of the town means "judgment of the people" and the church may be representative of the modern period.

THE LORD, 3:14

The risen Lord presents Himself to this church as the Amen (confirming all that He says), the faithful and true Witness in contrast to all the false prophets, and the beginning of the creation of God (indicating His priority over all creation, cf. Col. 1:17). He is the unalterable standard by which all must be measured.

CONDEMNATION, 3:15-17

Though outwardly this church must have appeared strong and prosperous, the Lord finds nothing to commend. His condemnation is severe against two things. (1) Gross indifference (vv. 15-16). Near Laodicea were hot mineral springs whose water could be drunk only if very hot. When lukewarm it became nauseating—as this church had become. (2) Spiritual poverty and self-deception (v. 17). The phrase "I am rich, and increased with goods" implies that the church was boasting of getting her wealth by her own effort. In reality she was poor, though she did not recognize her true state.

EXHORTATION, 3:18-19

The exhortation is for the church to find in Christ true riches ("gold tried in the fire"), unfeigned purity ("white raiment") and spiritual sight. The reference to eye salve alludes to the fact that Laodicea was a center for making medicines, one of which was a tablet to be powdered and smeared on the eyes.

PROMISES, 3:20-21

It seems unbelievable that Christ should be outside the door of His own church but this is exactly what verse 20 pictures. And yet He still extends His offer of grace to any individual who will invite Him into his heart. When the Saviour comes in He will take whatever the individual offers ("sup with him") and give to that individual all the riches that He has to offer ("and he with me"). Then to that believer is promised true exaltation in association with Christ in His rule (v. 21).

IV

THE THRONE IN HEAVEN
4:1-11

SECTION III: "THE THINGS WHICH SHALL BE HEREAFTER," 4:1—22:21

CHAPTER 4 begins the third principal section of the book, being introduced with the same words as were used in the outline in 1:19 ("hereafter," *meta tauta*). This entire portion is divided into three principal sections: the tribulation period (6:1—19:21); the millennium (20:1-15); and the eternal state (21:1—22:21). Chapters four and five form a prologue to the entire section. It was necessary that John be given a glimpse of the throne in heaven before witnessing the terrible judgments to be poured out on the earth. In other words, he was given a heavenly perspective on earthly events as he walked through the door that was opened to him in 4:1.

The word "door" is used only four times in the entire book. In 3:8 there is a door of opportunity for service for the church at Philadelphia. In 3:20 (where the word is used twice) the opening of the door of the heart brings salvation and fellowship. Here the door opened to John heavenly insights on this earthly scene, a most necessary prerequisite to understanding the purposes of God. The words "come up hither" indicate John's personal transferral from earth to heaven. They do not teach the rapture of the church, although in the pretribulational understanding of prophecy the rapture of the church would occur at this point in the book. In a posttribulational view, of course, the church remains on the earth during the entire tribulation period and is not raptured until immediately before the second coming in chapter 19.

PERSON ON THE THRONE, 4:2-3a

When John arrived in heaven he was immediately in the spirit (cf. 1:10) —a state of spiritual sensitivity in connection with receiving the visions. First he saw the throne. Revelation is a throne book, the word being used forty-five times as compared with only fifteen other occurrences of the word in the entire New Testament. The one sitting (present participle in both vv. 2 and 3, indicating continuous occupancy) on the throne is identified in verse 8 as God. He is described in terms of two precious stones. The jasper is explained in 21:11 as clear as crystal, that is, the color of light. The sardius stone, named for the city of Sardis where it was found, is blood red.

PICTURE CONNECTED WITH THE THRONE, 4:3b, 5-6a

AROUND THE THRONE, 3b

Around the throne was a rainbow the light green color of an emerald. The color may suggest a mediating between the brilliant colors of the jasper and sardius stones, but the rainbow itself was a vivid reminder of the faithfulness of God (Gen. 9:11-17). Unlike the sight of rainbows on earth of which we usually see only a part, this heavenly rainbow completely encircles the throne of God thus emphasizing the completeness of His faithfulness.

OUT OF THE THRONE, v. 5a

From the throne came lightnings, thunderings and voices. These seem to be portents of judgments and are found again in 8:5; 11:19 and 16:18.

BEFORE THE THRONE, VV. 5b-6

Before the throne were seven lamps of fire. They are interpreted as the seven spirits of God or the fullness of the Holy Spirit (as in 1:4; 3:1; 5:6). Also before the throne (the same preposition is used) was a sea of glasslike crystal. What John saw is comprehensible; its significance, though, may not be so clear. Swete thinks it "suggests the vast distance which, even in the case of one who stood at the door of heaven, intervened between himself and the Throne of God.* Strauss contrasts it with the laver in the tabernacle which was for cleansing. He notes that in heaven the sea is solidified, indicating that the saints have attained a fixed state of holiness (cf. 15:2).†

PERSONS AROUND THE THRONE, 4:4

CHARACTER

The persons around the throne are described as twenty-four elders. Some, such as W. R. Newell,‡ are convinced that these are twenty-four heavenly beings of an angelic order which is associated with God's government in some special way. Most other premillennial writers understand them to be twenty-four redeemed human beings around the throne who, though individuals, represent all the redeemed. This is not to say that there were not more than twenty-four around the throne, but it is to say that they represent all the redeemed. In the New Testament, elders as the highest officials in the church do represent the whole church (cf. Acts 15:6; 20:28), and in the Old Testament, twenty-four elders were appointed by King David to represent the entire Levitical priesthood (I Chron. 24). When those twenty-four elders met together in the temple precincts in Jerusalem, the entire priestly house was repre-

*Henry Barclay Swete, *The Apocalypse of St. John* (London: Macmillan, 1907), p. 70.
†Lehman Strauss, *The Book of the Revelation* (Neptune, N. J.: Loizeaux Bros., 1964), p. 134.
‡*The Book of the Revelation* (Chicago: Moody Press, n.d.), pp. 373-74.

sented. Thus it seems more likely that the elders represent redeemed human beings, not angels.

Some understand the twenty-four to be divided into two
groups of twelve each, one group representing the redeemed of
the Old Testament and the other the redeemed of the New
Testament church. Others do not include the Old Testament
saints at all but see the twenty-four elders as representing the
church only.§ This appears to be more probable, since redeemed Israelites will not be resurrected until the second coming. By either interpretation the church is included and is thus
in heaven before the tribulation begins.

CORONATION

The elders are seated on thrones (not "seats," as in the AV)
and are crowned with gold crowns. The word for crown (*stephanos*) is the same as used of the believers' rewards in I Corinthians 9:25; I Thessalonians 2:19; II Timothy 4:8; James
1:12; I Peter 5:4 and seems to indicate further that the twenty-
four elders are human, not angelic, beings. Actually, crowns
are never promised to angels.

CLOTHING

These saints are clothed in white raiment. This type of dress
is attributed to saints, not angels, elsewhere in Revelation (3:
5, 18).

PRAISE TO THE THRONE, 4:6*b*-11

LIVING ONES, vv. 6*b*-9

In verse 6 we are introduced to another group in connection
with the throne, the four "beasts." The translation is not good,
for the word means "living ones" and does not of itself indicate
whether they were animal, human, angelic or divine. Many believe that they are cherubim, since Ezekiel writes of living ones

§J. B. Smith, *A Revelation of Jesus Christ* (Scottdale, Pa.: Herald
Press, 1961), p. 106.

and identifies them as cherubim (Ezek. 10:15, 20). Others think these living ones are manifestations or attributes of God Himself who is on the throne. They are said to be "in the midst of" the throne—something not said about anyone or anything else in this chapter. But they are also said to be around the throne (as are the rainbow and the elders). Whatever they are may be obscure, but what they do is quite clear.

Each one is different in appearance. It would be difficult to ignore the similarity between the four living ones and the four-fold manner in which Christ is represented in the Gospels. "Like a lion" represents His kingship as particularly emphasized by Matthew. "Like a calf," that is, the sacrificial animal (Heb. 9:12, 19), reminds one of Mark's emphasis. "A face as a man" is obviously akin to Luke's emphasis on the humanity of Christ, and "a flying eagle" links Him with heaven, as John does.

The living ones' praise of God is ceaseless ("day and night"). They ascribe to God holiness (cf. Isa. 6:3), total authority ("Almighty" literally means "all-ruler"), eternality, glory and honor (v. 9). They also offer thanks to God. Glory and honor have to do with the perfections of God, while thanks refers to His gifts in creation and redemption.

TWENTY-FOUR ELDERS, vv. 10-11

The elders who have been seated on their thrones (cf. v. 4) rise and prostrate themselves before God. The word "worship" means to prostrate oneself before one whose worth is acknowledged (the English word worship was originally "worthship"). As a further act of homage they cast their crowns before God and praise Him in the words of verse 11. They address the One on the throne as the Lord and "our God" (in better texts, though omitted in the AV). They ascribe to Him glory, honor and power. They attribute to Him not only the creation of all things but the motivation for creating all things as being His own will (literally, "on account of thy will they are and were created"). His will is the cause of creation and He Himself is the Agent of it.

If the living ones are cherubim, then the scene is one of the redeemed (as represented by the twenty-four elders) joining with the cherubim (representing all the elect angels) in magnifying the worth of the Creator-God. If the living ones represent the attributes of God, then the elders are seen responding with worship to the revelation of God's attributes. In either case the glory of the elders falls before the glory of God, for all that we have as redeemed people is a gift of His grace according to the pleasure of His own will. In heaven we will acknowledge this. It is tragic that we do not do it sooner.

V

THE SEVEN-SEALED BOOK
5:1-14

CHAPTERS 4 and 5 are a unit since they describe the scene in heaven, which gave John the proper perspective on the judgments to follow. In chapter 4 the focus of attention is on the throne and its occupant; in chapter 5 it is on the book and its recipient.

DESCRIPTION OF THE BOOK, 5:1

POSITION

The book was in the right hand of God on the throne when John first saw it (though it was later removed from that place, v. 7).

CHARACTERISTICS

The book was probably a scroll rather than a codex (like our modern books) (cf. *biblion* in v. 1 with Luke 4:17, 20; II Tim. 4:13). It was sealed securely with seven seals which, if this was a scroll, would have been in a continuous line. Although the contents of the book were not then known, it was so full that the writing overflowed to the back side as well.

CONTENTS

Actually, we are not told in this chapter what the book contained, but when the seals are broken in chapter 6 the judgments of God are poured out on the earth. When the seventh seal is opened, the trumpets sound (8:1) and when the seventh trumpet blows, Christ is said to receive the kingdoms of this world (11:15).

Thus the book seems to contain the story of man's losing his lordship over creation and the regaining of that authority by the Man Christ Jesus. The book might be titled the "Book of Redemption" since it contains the story of redemption to its final consummation, not only in relation to man but also to the world. Satan had usurped what God originally gave to man in Adam, and Christ the Redeemer reclaimed cursed man and the cursed earth (cf. Heb. 2:5-9).

PROBLEM WITH THE BOOK, 5:2-5

PROBLEM, v. 2

A problem immediately arose. An angel asked who was worthy to open the book and break the seals.

REACTIONS, vv. 3-4

First there was a search which yielded no one able to open the book. The threefold characterization of the universe is the same as in Philippians 2:10. This failure to find any qualified person shows the complete moral inability of man.

Second, there was sorrow and sobbing on the part of John, because it appeared as if there were no one who could redeem the inheritance. The weeping continued (imperfect tense in v. 4) until one of the elders stopped John and announced that Christ would open the book. He is the Lion of the tribe of Judah (cf. Gen. 49:8-10) and the Root of David (Matt. 22:42-43). Both descriptions emphasize Christ's kingship as the noblest Son (lion) of the kingly tribe and as the One greater than King David who will fulfill the promises of the Davidic covenant.

RECIPIENT OF THE BOOK, 5:6-14

REVEALED, 6-7

The Lion is now revealed as a Lamb, but the fourfold description scarcely fits the usual image of a lamb!

The Lamb. He is *standing* in the midst of the throne. A standing lamb is a contradiction of ideas but well represents the majesty and meekness of the Lamb of God. In heaven the Lord is seen both as seated (in relation to the finished aspect of His work of redemption) and standing (in relation to the unfinished aspect of completing this redemption). Here He is standing ready to complete His work and assume the reins of power and government which are rightfully His.

The Lamb is slain. The emphasis is not on the crucifixion but on the resurrection since the slain Lamb is standing, not lying dead. This description also seems to indicate that the marks of His death remain unaltered throughout eternity to remind His people of the cost of their redemption.

The Lamb is strong. Horns are everywhere in the Bible a symbol of strength (I Kings 22:11; Zech. 1:18). Death has not weakened Him.

The Lamb is searching in wisdom. His seven eyes represent the fullness of the Spirit of God. It is this One who, not as an interloper but as the legitimate Heir, takes the book out of the hand of God on the throne. This is one of the most climactic acts in all history, for it assures the regaining of all that was lost.

REVERED, 8-14

At this point all creation bursts into praise for the Lamb who can open the book.

By the twenty-four elders, vv. 8-10, 14.

1. Their actions. The elders fall before the throne and worship (same word as in 4:10) the Lamb.

2. Their implements. They have harps or lyres, the tra-

ditional instruments for praise (Ps. 33:2; 98:5) , and with
the prayers of the saints offered as incense in bowls (an
open vessel more like a saucer) . The gender of the participle "having" shows that the harps and bowls are used
only by the elders and not by the living ones.

3. Their song. Their song magnifies the worth of the Lamb
   for four reasons.

   a. He was slain.

   b. That death ("by thy blood") brought redemption to
   people from every kindred, tongue, people and nation.

   c. That redemption also resulted in a position before
   God as a kingdom and priests (cf. 1:5-6; 20:6) .

   d. In the future (though some texts have a present tense
   of the verb here) the redeemed will reign on the
   earth—a reference to our participation in the millennial kingdom. In verses 9-10 there is also a textual
   problem as to whether the pronouns ought to be "us"
   or "them." If "us," then the elders are obviously
   singing of their own redemption (and of those whom
   they represent) ; if "them," then they still could be
   singing of their own redemption in the third person
   instead of the first (as Exodus 15:13, 15-17) .

By angels, vv. 11-12. The angels (who are clearly distinguished here from the elders, indicating that the latter are not
angels) join in praise to the Lamb. Nowhere in the Bible
is it directly said that angels sing. Here they cry with a loud
voice. Their number is an innumerable multitude. They do
not directly address the Lamb as did the elders, but they give
to Him a sevenfold ascription of praise.

By every creature, v. 13. Every creature joins in the ascription of praise (Phil. 2:8-11) .

By the living ones, v. 14. The four living ones respond to
this hymn of adoration with an "amen," closing this scene of
universal homage to the One who is the focus of all God's purposes for time and eternity.

VI

THE SIX SEALS

6:1-17

ACCORDING TO THE OUTLINE of the book, the third and last
principal section begins with 4:1, but chapters 4 and 5 constitute a prologue to the action which begins with chapter 6.
Chapters 6–19 concern the events of the tribulation period,
climaxing with the second coming of Christ in 19:11-16. There
is no problem in outlining the events of these chapters; the
difficulty comes in determining the sequential order of those
events, particularly the relation of the three series of judgments to each other. Do the judgments of the seals (chap. 6),
and of the trumpets (chaps. 8–9) and of the bowls (chap. 16)
follow each other in succession, or do the trumpets and/or the
bowls recapitulate the judgments of the seals with greater intensity? In other words, do the trumpet and bowl judgments
follow the seals as different and distinct judgments or do they
picture the same judgments? To this writer's understanding
they all follow in chronological sequence and there is no recapitulation.* In this book the chronological sequence is based
on the premise that the judgments are in order and that chapters 6, 8–9 and 16 form the chronological backbone of this
section.

The other chapters in this section (besides 6, 8–9 and 16)

*For a demonstration of the validity of the view that the trumpets do
not recapitulate the bowls and that the trumpets and bowls do not recapitulate the seals see Wilbur M. Smith, "Revelation," *The Wycliffe
Bible Commentary* (Chicago: Moody Press, 1962), p. 1516.

relate events most important to our understanding of the tribulation period but not necessarily in chronological order. Some commentators call them parentheses, which is a satisfactory word as long as it does not connote unrelatedness or unimportance. These chapters contain fill-in material which is vital to the complete picture but not necessarily arranged chronologically.

To summarize: Chapters 6—19, which picture the tribulation period, contain three series of judgments—the seals (6), the trumpets (8—9) and the bowls (16). These follow one another in sequence. The other chapters reveal vital information about the period but are not arranged in chronological order. They either cover the entire period, or spotlight an event within the period, or survey the first or last half of the period. The chapters in this section are arranged like a conversation on the telephone between two persons. They start telling the story in order (chap. 6) but soon there is an interruption to fill in some information (chap. 7). Then the order of events is resumed (chaps. 8—9), then some more fill-in (chaps. 10—15). There is a return to the progressive order of events (chap. 16) and finally more detail (chaps. 17—19). Sometimes the fill-in runs ahead of the story and at other times it backs up to add or emphasize pertinent information. It may be helpful at this point to recapitulate the outline of Revelation used in this book.

    I. "The things which thou hast seen" (1:1-20)
   II. "The things which are" (2:1—3:22)
  III. "The things which shall be hereafter" (4:1—22:21)
        Prologue (4:1—22:21)
     A. The Tribulation (6:1—19:21)
       1. Seal Judgments (6:1-17)
       2. Trumpet Judgments (8:1—9:21)
       3. Bowl Judgments (16:1-21)
     B. The Millennium (20:1-15)
     C. The Eternal State (21:1—22:21)

First Seal, 6:1-2

The first seal is opened by the Lamb, and the wrath of the usually docile Lamb begins to be revealed. The opening of the first seal reveals to John a white horse and rider. Some interpret the rider of the white horse as Christ because of 19:11, but the only similarity between the two passages is the white horse. Other judgments do not follow in chapter 19 as they do in chapter 6; the crown which the rider wears in 6:2 (*stephanos*) is different from that in 19:12 (*diadema*) ; and the appearance of Christ on earth at this point in the book is incongruous. The rider is Antichrist who goes forth conquering at the very beginning of the tribulation period. The method of conquest, however, does not seem to be by open hostilities, for peace is not removed from the earth until the second seal. One might label this judgment, then, "cold war," and this corresponds perfectly with the picture of delusion described in I Thessalonians 5:3.

Second Seal, 6:3-4

In interpreting this book it is always a wise procedure to move from the clear statements to the less clear. It is perfectly clear that, in the judgment of the second seal, peace is removed from the earth and men begin open war with each other. Phrases in verse 4 so state, and the phrase "there was given unto him a great sword" confirms it. The red color of the horse also suggests bloodshed.

Third Seal, 6:5-6

The third judgment brings famine to the world. The black horse forebodes death, and the pair of balances bespeaks a careful rationing of food. Normally a "penny" (a Roman *denarius,* a day's wages in Palestine in Jesus' day, Matt. 20:2) would buy eight measures of wheat or twenty-four of barley. Under these famine conditions the same wage will buy only one measure of wheat or three of barley. In other words, there

will be one-eighth of the normal supply of food. The phrase
"see thou hurt not the oil and the wine" is an ironic twist in
this terrible situation. Apparently luxury food items will not
be in short supply, but of course most people will not be able
to afford them. This situation will only serve to taunt the
populace in their impoverished state.

Fourth Seal, 6:7-8

The color of the fourth horse is "pale" or better, "yellowish-
green." The same word is used in 9:4 of green vegetation. This
one alone among the four horsemen is named, and he is called
Death. Death claims the physical part of man (the immaterial never dies) and is accompanied by Hades (Hell) which
claims the immaterial part. Here is evidence that death does
not end all, for the soul goes to Hades and eventually the unsaved person will be cast into the lake of fire (20:14). The
effect of this judgment is that one-fourth of the population of
the earth is killed (cf. 9:18 where an additional one-third are
killed). The means of extermination are four: sword (war),
hunger (famine that often follows war), death (perhaps by
plagues of diseases which often accompany war) and wild
beasts of the earth (which apparently will be unrestrained and
will roam to kill men). Suddenly all of man's programs for
bringing in peace, plenty and longevity through medicine will
be overturned in the short time that it will take to accomplish
this judgment (cf. Matt. 24:4-7).

Fifth Seal, 6:9-11

The fifth seal depicts action in heaven which presupposes
certain happenings on earth. Attention has previously been
focused on events which will occur on the earth. Now it shifts
to a group of martyrs in heaven, and, of course, they are in
heaven because of having been martyred on the earth. Who
are these people? They are not the martyrs of the Church Age,
for they were raptured before the holocaust of the tribulation
began. They must be those martyred during these first months

of the tribulation when the judgments of the first four seals were being poured out. The reason for their being slain is plain: "for the word of God, and for the testimony which they held" (v. 9*b*). Literally, the text says "for the witness which they were having [imperfect tense]." In other words, they are faithful witnesses during the early days of the tribulation when men are going to be judged by God but will not turn to Him. In their wrath the vile men kill God's witnesses.

As soon as they die they are received into heaven, and they are pictured here to John as under the altar (i.e., they had already been offered as a sacrifice). They wear white robes (cf. 7:9; 19:8) signifying their fully redeemed state, and they cry for vengeance on those who killed them. They address the Lord as Despot (v. 10), a word which shows recognition of His absolute control over all the affairs of the world. The Lord's answer to them (v. 11) is that they should wait a little while for vengeance until certain others should be martyred also. God's reply provides a glimpse into the complicated problem of why evil is allowed to reign. God simply allows it for His own purposes, which are best from the viewpoint of His total plan, though difficult to understand from our limited viewpoint. It was difficult for these martyrs to understand why God would allow these evil murderers to live, but He asks them to trust Him to be working out all things in the best way.

SIXTH SEAL, 6:12-17

Apparently following immediately, the judgment of the sixth seal unleashes universal havoc on the earth. Six catastrophic events will be involved: (1) A single great earthquake will occur. (2) The sun will be darkened so that it becomes black as sackcloth. It is very important to notice the words "as" and "like" and the phrase "as it were" in interpreting the book. The sun will not be turned into sackcloth but will be blackened *as* sackcloth. (3) The moon will be reddened *as* blood. (4) There will be a meteor shower on the earth with

resultant devastation. (5) Apparently heaven will be opened
for a moment so that men on earth can have a glimpse of that
awesome scene with God on the throne. (6) Every mountain
and island will be moved to some extent. There is no "as" in
this sentence.

The result of these judgments will be to strike terror into
the hearts of men living on the earth. It is most interesting to
note that what strikes fear in them will not be so much the
physical disturbance in the heavens or earth as the sight of
God on the throne. Men will plead to be hidden "from the
face of him that sitteth on the throne, and from the wrath of
the Lamb." They will go to any lengths to avoid God, even to
seeking death from the rocks and mountains where they hide.
This judgment has effects in all the world and among all
classes of people (v. 15). At this point men will know as-
suredly that the tribulation has begun, for they recognize it as
the "great day of his wrath" (v. 17). There seems to be no general turning *to* God in repentance with a plea for mercy, but
only a turning *from* the face of God.

Two characteristics of the tribulation days distinguish that
period from all other periods of trouble and persecution that
have come or will come upon the earth. The first is that the
judgments of the tribulation are to be worldwide. All kinds
of people throughout the earth (righteous remnant, sinners
and all social classes) will feel the judgments of that period.
Also, when the tribulation comes, men will not only know that
the end of the world is near, but they will act like it. In every
age there are men who predict the end of the world, but in no
age have men acted as if they believed it. When the tribulation comes, men will not be concerned with buying and selling
real estate or saving and planning for the future; according to
these verses they will dig out caves in the mountains and rocks
and seek death, not the prolonging of life. This is an awesome
scene, but if language means anything, the very details are
plain.

VII

THE REDEEMED OF THE TRIBULATION

7:1-17

THE NARRATIVE SEQUENCE is interrupted at this point in Revelation, for chapter 6 closed with a description of the sixth seal and the seventh seal is not opened until the beginning of chapter 8. Although in a sense chapter 7 is a parenthesis, it is also a very logical interlude in the account. From the severity of the judgments under the sixth seal it would appear that not a single person could or would be saved. "For the great day of his wrath is come; and who shall be able to stand?" But even in the wrath of the tribulation God remembers mercy, so this scene of judgment is interrupted by the scene of mercy in this chapter.

SEALING OF 144,000 JEWS, 7:1-8

SUSPENSION OF JUDGMENT, 7:1-3

Instruments of the suspension, vv. 1-2. In suspending judgment for a time God will use angels. Scarcely any person appreciates the extent of the ministry of angels. It is not that God requires their services, but He chooses to use them in the execution of His plans. In Revelation angels are used both in executing judgments (as in 8:2) and in staying judgment (as here in 7:1-3). In addition to the reference to the angels of the churches in Revelation 2—3 (which may be angels or human messengers) , there are sixty-seven other occurrences of the word in this book.

John first saw four angels who apparently control the winds (cf. the angel of fire, 14:18, and the angel of the waters, 16:5) . Their mission at this time will be to prevent an outbreak of fury of the elements. Very soon such an outbreak will occur, and it will affect the trees which are mentioned in verse 1 as being protected then (cf. 8:7) . Then John saw a fifth angel who came from the east (literally, the rising of the sun) . He was also given a special mission in relation to the 144,000.

Instruction concerning suspension, vv. 2-3. This fifth angel appears to be a superior to the other four. This is not strange. for other Scriptures demonstrate that there are ranks among both the good and evil angels (Eph. 3:10; 6:12) . He instructs the four to suspend judgment, but he also associates them with him in the sealing ("till *we* have sealed," v. 3*b*) . His crying with a loud voice may emphasize the urgency of this project. The instructions are clear: Suspend judgment for a time.

Intent of the suspension, v. 3. The purpose of the suspension is that a certain group may be sealed. These are designated "the servants of our God." Who they are is described in detail in verses 4-8. They are Jews from each of the twelve tribes, and they do some particular service for God. In some way they are sealed. Whether a visible mark or characteristic of some kind is involved is not stated or implied in the text. Some suggest something visible after the manner of Ezekiel 9:4 or like the glory with which Moses' face shone. But a seal does not have to be visible to be real (Eph. 4:30) . It is principally a guarantee of ownership and security, and both these ideas are evident in the sealing of these 144,000. They are owned by God, which means they are redeemed people. And they are kept secure by God, which means they have physical safety from their enemies on the earth while they are accomplishing their service for the Lord.

SUM OF THE JEWS, 7:4-8

Although some interpret this list very generally as preservation during trials, and others as the sealing of the church, if language is to be understood normally, the list is of 144,000 Jews. The repetitious "of the tribe of . . . were sealed" is too ringing to allow any other conclusion. Anyone today who would claim to be among this group would have to know to what tribe he belonged. J. A. Seiss wrote:

> Nor is there a vice or device of sacred hermeneutics, which so beclouds the Scriptures, and so unsettles the faith of men, as this constant attempt to read *Church* for *Israel*, and Christian peoples for Jewish tribes. As I read the Bible, when God says *"children of Israel,"* I do not understand Him to mean any but people of Jewish blood, be they Christians or not; and when He speaks of the twelve tribes of the sons of Jacob, and gives the names of the tribes, it is impossible for me to believe that He means the Gentiles, in any sense or degree, whether they be believers or not.*

The identification is no problem if the language is understood plainly. But there are three problems in this list. The first is the inclusion of Levi among the twelve tribes. Normally Levi, being the priestly tribe, was considered to have no inheritance among the twelve tribes. Perhaps he is included here because the priestly functions ceased with the coming of Christ. The second is the mention of Joseph instead of Ephraim. Normally Manasseh and Ephraim are both mentioned since they both received an equal portion of territory along with the rest of the tribes. Of course, a double number is counted in this list, but under the names of Joseph and Manasseh rather than Ephraim and Manasseh.

The third problem concerns the omission of Dan from this list, something that was necessary if Levi were to be included.

*J. A. Seiss, *The Apocalypse* (Grand Rapids: Zondervan Pub. House, 1865), I, 405-6.

The usual reason given for this omission is that Dan was guilty of idolatry on many occasions (Lev. 24:11; Judges 18:1-2, 30-31; I Kings 12:28). The same reason is often given for the omission of Ephraim. It has been suggested further that the antichrist may come from this tribe and that this accounts for its omission from this list (cf. Gen. 49:17; Jer. 8:16). Whatever the reason for Dan's omission from the tribes from which the 144,000 elect will come, this is not the end of God's dealings with that tribe. The Danites will receive a portion of the land during the millennial kingdom. Indeed, in Ezekiel 48:1 Dan heads the list of the tribes as the inheritance is divided to them (cf. also v. 32). So the exclusion of Revelation is not permanent, for the gifts and calling of God with regard to His people, including Dan, are without repentance.

SAVING OF MANY GENTILES, 7:9-17

PERSONS SAVED, 7:9

Their number. Verse 9 introduces a new vision with the words "after these things." John saw a group different in several ways from the 144,000. This group he described literally as "a great crowd." This is an innumerable group, not a definite number like the 144,000.

Their nationalities. The 144,000 are all Israelites. This group is composed of many nationalities. Redeemed Jews are evidently included since the word "kindreds" is literally "tribes."

Their nature. They are described as wearing white robes and holding palms in their hands. In other words, they are redeemed and rejoicing. The word for robes is stoles—white stoles finer than the finest white ermine or mink and indicative of a far more important possession, salvation. The palms apparently denote rejoicing and victory (cf. John 12:13 for the only other occurrence in the New Testament and cf. Neh. 8:17).

PRAISE FOR SALVATION, 7:10-12

The redeemed multitude cry an ascription of praise to God and to the Lamb for their salvation (v. 10). The angels, the four living ones and the elders respond by worshiping God. The angels, of course, do not personally experience salvation, but they rejoice in the salvation of sinners (cf. Luke 15:8-10).

PERIOD OF SALVATION, 7:13-14

John was evidently puzzling over the identity of this group (scarcely imaginable if the group were the church saints), and God who knows our thoughts answered his perplexity through one of the elders. They are explicitly identified as those who came out of "the tribulation, the great one."

> That they are distinct from the church appears from the following considerations: Those were kept out of the great tribulation (3:10); these came out. Those wear white raiment; these white robes. Those sit on thrones round about the throne; these stand before the throne. Those wear crowns; these are uncrowned. Those have harps and vials; these have palms in their hands. Those sing a new song; these cry with a loud voice. Those are kings and priests and reign with Him; these serve Him day and night.†

Many of these will doubtless be saved through believing the message which the 144,000 preach during the tribulation days.

PROVISIONS OF SALVATION, 7:15-17

Service, v. 15. This group (along with others) will serve God. "In his temple" likely indicates some special service for them in the millennial temple.

Satisfaction, vv. 15-16. They are satisfied because of the presence of God. The phrase that begins "he that sitteth" literally reads, "he that sitteth on the throne shall spread his tent over

†J. B. Smith, *A Revelation of Jesus Christ* (Scottdale, Pa.: Herald Press, 1961), p. 135.

them." God's sheltering, shepherdly, protecting care is their portion. They are satisfied because of the provisions of God (v. 16), which include no hunger, no thirst, no exposure.

Sufficiency, v. 17. Sufficiency from the shepherding ministry of the Lamb is the final provision of their salvation mentioned in this chapter. The word translated "feed" is literally "shepherd." The word "living" is in an emphatic position making the phrase read "life's water-springs," and the mention of eternal life brings the additional assurance of no tears. The Lamb in this scene is not only the satisfaction and sufficiency of these redeemed but His presence is security. In turn the redeemed serve Him without interruption.

Both these groups in Revelation 7, the 144,000 and the saved multitude who are largely Gentiles, demonstrate clearly that the tribulation will be a period of much salvation. Even though the body of saints known as the church will be completed and raptured and thus the Holy Spirit's residence in the world will in a special sense be withdrawn, God will not cease to save men who believe in His Son. The activity of the grace of God will not cease as long as time continues.

VIII

THE FIRST FOUR TRUMPETS

8:1-13

THE INTERLUDE recorded in chapter 7 has concluded and the pouring out of judgments on the earth resumes.

OPENING OF THE SEVENTH SEAL, 8:1

With the opening of this last seal the book is now fully opened, and one would expect a holocaust to let loose. Instead there is silence. All of the choruses of the elders and the cries of the angels cease. The stillness is so intense that it can be felt. This is a silence of expectancy, for this is the last seal. It is also a silence of foreboding that precedes the onslaught of judgments. It lasts for half an hour (which may be understood just as literally as the other time designations in the book). Silence at this point, after all the vocal expressions of worship previously noted, would be an awesome thing.

With the opening of this seal comes the series of trumpet judgments. It has already been noted that some interpreters consider these series of judgments successive, in which case the trumpets come out of and follow the seals. Others feel that there is overlapping and recapitulation.* It seems to this writer that the simplest understanding of these verses favors the successive idea.

°J. B. Smith, *A Revelation of Jesus Christ* (Scottdale, Pa.: Herald Press, 1961), p. 136.

EIGHT ANGELS, 8:2-6

PRESENCE ANGELS, VV. 2, 6

Their relationship. John first saw seven angels. They are a distinct group (the definite article is used) and they are before, or in the presence of, God. With the introduction of these angels no further mention is made of the seven spirits of God, which further indicates their special relationship to God and His purposes. (Could one of them be Gabriel, cf. Luke 1:13?)

Their responsibility. They are responsible for announcing the trumpet judgments. This responsibility is given to them, for the trumpets are given them (v. 2). The sounding of trumpets is always followed by something of outstanding importance. The first occurrence was at the giving of the law (Exodus 19:16; 20:18; cf. Jer. 4:5; I Cor. 15:51-52; I Thess. 4:16).

PRIEST ANGEL, VV. 3-5

Before the sounding of the trumpets an interlude occurs with the appearance of another angel. His function as a priest is clear; his identification is less sure. Some understand this to be Christ, our High Priest.† Others regard him as an angel,‡ and there seems to be no reason why an angel could not perform the functions described here. He adds incense to the prayers of the saints that ascend before God. Though the imagery is of the tabernacle worship, the meaning is now apparent in light of the finished work of Christ. The incense is the sweet savor of His life and work which gives efficacy to the prayers of the saints.

Who are the saints whose prayers are being heard here? At the very least they are the saints of the tribulation days who

†Walter Scott, *Exposition of the Revelation of Jesus Christ* (London: Pickering & Inglis, n.d.), p. 180.
‡William R. Newell, *The Book of the Revelation* (Chicago: Moody Press, n.d.), p. 121.

are living on the earth and who pray to God for an outpouring of His wrath on the godless on the earth. But they may include the saints of all time whose longing petitions for the coming of the kingdom of the Lord are now about to be answered. In any case, their prayers are heard, angels being involved in the hearing and answering but all on the basis of the merit of the Saviour.

After prayer ascends, judgment descends (v. 5). The angel fills his censer with fire from the altar (not the golden altar before the throne but the brazen altar of judgment), and he casts it into the earth. There follows a token judgment—voices, thunderings, lightnings and an earthquake—a foretaste of the trumpet judgments to follow. The action of the priest angel gives the signal to the presence angels to sound the trumpets.

FIRST FOUR TRUMPETS, 8:7-13

FIRST TRUMPET, V. 7

The first trumpet will bring hail and fire mingled with blood on the earth. The result will be the burning of a third part of the earth (reliable texts insert this phrase in v. 7), a third part of the trees and all the grass. Commentators who hold to the futuristic interpretations of this book are divided over the extent to which these judgments should be understood plainly. Some see the words "trees," "grass," "sea" and "ships" as symbols. For instance, Walter Scott understands the third part of the earth to mean the devastation of the Western confederation of nations, the third part of the trees to be the leaders and great men of the world, and the grass to represent people in general. Of course, symbols are often used in this book, but they are so stated. Here there is no indication that these are symbols, so it seems better to understand them plainly.

It goes without saying that this question is not the question of literal versus figurative interpretation. It is a question of the extent to which symbols are being used within the framework of literal or plain interpretation of the book. Consistent interpretation in relation to the language of these verses would seem to rule out any symbols here. As has often been pointed out, it would be very inconsistent to understand these judgments symbolically and interpret the plagues in Egypt plainly and actually. The judgment of the first trumpet presents a grim picture of devastation on the vegetation of the world.

SECOND TRUMPET, VV. 8-9

The instrument of the second judgment is described with a figure—"as it were a great mountain burning with fire." It is not necessary to attempt to find something in the realm of experience which can match this description. John really does not say what the instrument of judgment will be, but he clearly reveals the effect of the judgment. A third part of the sea will become blood, causing the death of a third part of the life in the sea and the destruction of a third part of the shipping of the world. The far-reaching implications of such judgments are staggering to the mind.

THIRD TRUMPET, VV. 10-11

The judgment of the third trumpet affects the fresh water supply of the world. It will become bitter with the result that many will die. The instrument of judgment will be a great star which is labeled Wormwood. "Many species of wormwood grow in Palestine. . . . All species have a strong, bitter taste, leading to the use of the plant as a symbol of bitterness, sorrow, and calamity."§

FOURTH TRUMPET, VV. 12-13

The fourth judgment will affect the sun, moon, stars, and the uniformity of the day-night cycle. The sun, moon and

§J. D. Douglas (ed.), *The New Bible Dictionary* (Grand Rapids: Wm. B. Eerdmans Pub. Co., 1962), p. 1340.

stars will be smitten to the extent of one-third with the result that apparently the twenty-four-hour cycle will be shortened to a sixteen-hour cycle. The Lord Himself predicted in the Olivet discourse these "signs in the sun, and in the moon, and in the stars" (Luke 21:25). Perhaps this shortening of the days and nights is what is referred to in Matthew 24:22 (though, of course, that verse may mean that the total number of days is shortened).

At this point John heard and saw an eagle (not "angel" as in AV) announcing woes to come. These will be inflicted on "those dwelling on the earth." The means of punishment will be the last three trumpets of the angels which were yet to sound. Terrible as the first four trumpet judgments will be, the last three will be worse and are thus designated "woes."

> The warning is that trumpets five, six and seven will bring a new quality and degree of divine displeasure and consequent disaster. We shall see the first woe in the locusts (9:1-11); the second, in the Euphrates horsemen and hosts (9:13-21) and the plagues wherewith the two witnesses (11:5, 6) smite the earth. The third we see in the handing over of the earth to the Beast-worship of chapter 13—worst by far, of all! ‖

‖Newell, *op. cit.*, p. 127.

IX

WOES ON THE EARTH
9:1-21

LIKE ARROWS FROM A BOW the locusts of judgment of the first woe are discharged upon the earth.

Agent who discharged them, v. 1. When the fifth trumpet angel sounded, John saw a star. He is described as having fallen (not "fall" as AV) to the earth. In other words, John did not see the star actually fall; it was already fallen. Who or what is this star? Sometimes the word "star" refers to a heavenly body (as in 8:12). But the word is often used to refer to some kind of intelligent creature, usually an angel (cf. 1:20; Job 38:7). Both meanings are perfectly consistent with plain, normal interpretation. In English we use this word in the same two ways. Literally, a star means an astronomical entity; and equally literally, though as a figure of speech, we use the word to mean a person, like the star of a football game. Here the star is an intelligent creature who performs certain responsible actions.

Can the creature be identified further? He is obviously a creature with great authority to be able to hold captive and then unleash these locusts. He apparently is the same creature who in verse 11 is called the "angel of the bottomless pit," and that identifies him as Satan. This, of course, accords with the fact that he has fallen from heaven to the earth (Isa. 14:12-15; Luke 10:18). Although his great authority extends to having a key to the bottomless pit, it is comforting to remember that his power is delegated to him by God and restricted by the One who has the keys of death and of hades (1:18) and who eventually will confine Satan to that same bottomless pit (20:3).

Area from which they are discharged, v. 2. They come from this bottomless pit. Literally the phrase is "shaft of the abyss" in both verses 1 and 2. The word "abyss" occurs in Revelation seven times (9:1-2, 11; 11:7; 17:8; 20:1, 3) and elsewhere only twice (Luke 8:31; Rom. 10:7). The use of the word "shaft" gives the picture of a pit entered by a shaft or well which is guarded under lock and key. Luke 8:31 shows that the abyss is the abode of the demons. When the angel-star Satan opens the pit, smoke ascends *as* the smoke from a great furnace. In this chapter there are more occurrences of the words "as" and "like" than in any other chapter in the Bible, which shows how difficult it was for John to describe the scene which he saw in the vision. So dense was the smoke that the sun and air were darkened.

DESTRUCTION BY LOCUSTS, VV. 3-6

Out of the smoke came locusts onto the earth. The description which follows in verses 6-11 shows that these will not be ordinary locusts, and their origin from the shaft of the abyss substantiates that conclusion. These creatures are described as being very real so we must not consider them as merely "symbolic representations of judgment." They are animal creatures, like locusts, though not ordinary locusts, for they are demonic in nature. Indeed, it would be better to describe them as demons who take the form of these unique locusts. Verse 11 makes it clear that this is the case.

Its description, v. 3. The destruction which these demon-insects inflict is described like that of scorpions.

The pain from the sting of a scorpion, though not generally fatal, is, perhaps, the intensest that any animal can inflict upon the human body. The insect itself is the most
irascible and malignant that lives, and its poison is like
itself. Of a boy stung in the foot by a scorpion [it was
related that] . . . he rolled on the ground, grinding his
teeth, and foaming at the mouth. It was a long time before his complainings moderated, and even then he could
make no use of his foot, which was greatly inflamed. And
such is the nature of the torment which these locusts from
the pit inflict. They are also difficult to be guarded
against, if they can be warded off at all, because they fly
where they please, dart through the air, and dwell in
darkness.*

Limitation, vv. 4-5. Horrible as the torment will be, God
will place certain limitations on the activity of these demons.
They will be limited as to *what* they may strike and as to
how far they may go and as to *how long* they may do what
they will do. They will not attack the vegetation of the earth
(as common locusts do) ; they may only attack certain men,
that is, those who have not the seal of God in their foreheads
(the 144,000, cf. 7:3). The wicked will persecute God's servants, the 144,000; but in turn they will be tormented by this
plague which God allows. The demon-locusts will also be
limited in that they may not kill men, just torment them.
Further, the duration of this plague will be five months (cf. v.
10).

Effect, v. 6. The effect of this torment is to drive men to
suicide, but they will not be able to die. Although men will
prefer death to the agony of living, death will not be possible.
Bodies will not sink and drown; poisons and pills will have no
effect; and somehow even bullets and knives will not do their
intended job.

*J. A. Seiss, *The Apocalypse* (Grand Rapids: Zondervan Pub. House,
1865), II, 83.

DESCRIPTION OF LOCUSTS, VV. 7-12

John now attempts to describe these uncommon locusts, and these verses abound with the words of comparison: as and like.

Likeness, vv. 7-10. There are eight parts to the description which begins at the head and progresses backward to the tail. Overall they are like horses prepared for battle (cf. Joel 2:4). On their heads were *as it were* crowns of gold. Their faces were *as* the faces of men; their hair *as* the hair of women; their teeth *as* those of lions. They had breastplates *as it were* of iron and the sound of their wings was *as* chariots of horses going to battle. Finally, the scorpionlike sting of their tails is mentioned again along with the fact that this will be permitted to last only five months. Though it may be difficult for anyone to think of such creatures, that is no reason for understanding them as merely symbols. The power of demons is very great, and these uncommon locusts are demonic. Whatever the size and appearance of these creatures, one thing stands out in this description—they are ferocious. Little wonder this is called the first woe.

Although this judgment is literally hell on earth, the overruling power of God is interwoven throughout this passage. He allows this judgment to occur; He sets the limits on the destructive power of these locusts; He brings it to a conclusion when His purpose in it is finished. He is in complete control.

Leader, v. 11. These creatures are led in their work by a king, Satan. His name is given in both Hebrew and Greek and means "destroyer" in both languages. In this judgment he, through his demons, will attempt to destroy men's bodies; he also destroys the souls of those who refuse to receive the Saviour.

SECOND WOE—SIXTH TRUMPET, 9:13-21

COMMAND, VV. 13-15

When the sixth angel sounded, a voice from the golden altar gave the command to him concerning this second woe.

The golden altar is mentioned only here and in 8:3, and presumably the voice here in verse 13 belonged to the same priest angel introduced in 8:3. He commands the trumpet angel to loose four angels which were bound and continue so to be (the tense is perfect) in the river Euphrates. Here are four good angels under the command of the priest angel loosing four evil angels who up to this time had been bound in the Euphrates. These evil angels were prepared for the hour (the definite article is in the text in v. 15) and for the purpose (Greek, *hina*) of killing a third of the human race. Again, one sees the sovereign hand of God working all these events for His own glory and in His own time. These demons who had been kept for this hour could not have released themselves or been freed by Satan until God gave the command.

Under the fourth seal judgment (6:4) one-fourth of the earth had been slain; now one-third. This means that these two judgments alone (to say nothing of the death caused by other wars, etc.) have reduced the population of the earth by one-half.

COUNT, v. 16

An immense army of horsemen appear at this point, and the total number of them is 200,000,000. This army might be composed of human beings and it might equally well be an army of demons. There are other examples in Scripture of supernatural armies (II Kings 2:11; 6:13-17; Rev. 19:14). The weapons of this army are fire, smoke and brimstone (v. 17) which are weapons of hell and may further indicate that the army is made up of the inhabitants of hell—demons.

CHARACTERISTICS, v. 17

The horses had heads like lions and tails like serpents (v. 19). The riders had breastplates of fire, jacinth (a blue stone) and brimstone. From the mouths of the horses came fire, smoke and brimstone, the weapons of destruction.

CONSEQUENCES, vv. 18-21

"By these three" should read "by these three plagues"; that is, the fire, smoke and brimstone (sulphur). The first consequence of the activity of this army from hell is that one-third of the population is destroyed. The second consequence concerns those who were not killed. One would expect that in the midst of all this suffering, men would turn to God and cry out for mercy. Instead, we read that they repented not. In verses 20 and 21 is a description of the religion and life of unredeemed man on the earth during these tribulation days. His religion will be the worship of demons (cf. I Tim. 4:1) and idols. His life will be filled with murder, sorcery, fornication and stealing. From the word for sorcery we derive in English the word "pharmacy." Sorceries, then, must include the misuse of drugs. Notice that three of these four practices are direct violations of three of the Ten Commandments (murder, fornication, stealing) . Vice will reign in the place of virtue, as is always the case since man's religion determines his ethics. People in these days will have religion with many of its visible representations, but it will do nothing to change their lives.

X

THE ANGEL AND THE LITTLE
OPENED BOOK

10:1-11

CHARACTER OF THE ANGEL, 10:1-2

THE VISION which John received at this point is the longest in
the book. Notice that the words "I saw" do not appear again
until 13:1. This section also forms the longest interlude between judgments. Between the sixth and seventh seals came
the sealing of the 144,000 and the salvation of the great multitude. Here, between the sixth and seventh trumpets, come a
number of revelations before the sounding of that last trumpet.

The appearance of this angel must have been spectacular to
John, for the angel had a number of unusual characteristics.
(1) His origin was heavenly (v. 1). (2) He was glorious in
appearance (v. 1) —clothed with a cloud (often connected with
the appearance of someone from heaven, Dan. 7:13; I Thess.
4:17) ; a rainbow on his head (as a crown) ; face as the sun in
its brilliance; and feet as pillars in their stance. (3) The angel
held a little book opened in his hand (v. 2). The form of the
word "open" in verse 2 is perfect passive, indicating that the
book had been already opened before it appeared at this point.
This would indicate that this is not the same book as was seen
sealed in chapter 5. The contents are revealed later in this
chapter. (4) The angel took a stand with one foot on the

sea and the other on the land (v. 2). This seems to present an image of conquest and to relate the angel and his ministry to God's purpose of taking possession of the entire world (land and sea), which will be worked out in the tribulation period.

What do these characteristics tell us about the identity of this angel? Some identify him with the Lord Jesus. The descent in a cloud (cf. Ps. 104:3), the face as the sun (cf. 1:16), the feet as pillars of fire (cf. 1:15), the planting of his feet in an act of taking possession (I Cor. 10:26) all point to the angel being Christ. Others, however, point out that an angel might have these characteristics as well. He is called a "mighty" angel (the same word as in 5:2). Similar characteristics are ascribed to a man (clearly an angelic being) in Daniel 10:5 ff. Furthermore, the archangel Michael's name means "who is like God," which would make these characteristics not unexpected. Also, there might be some problem in a descent of Christ at this point in the book (v. 1). There would be no problem if this were an angel. If this is an angel it is quite possible that he is the same one that appeared in 8:3, the word "another" in 10:1 merely distinguishing him from the seven trumpet angels as it does in 8:3. In either identification he is a mighty being with great power and authority, whether His own as Christ or delegated to him as a mighty angel for use in accomplishing God's program.

CRY OF THE ANGEL, 10:3-4

CHARACTER

The cry was with a loud voice like the roaring of a lion. The metaphor emphasizes the strength of the angel's voice.

CONSEQUENCES

Two things followed. First, seven thunders uttered their voices, and second, John was restrained from revealing what the thunders said. Thunders are usually harbingers of coming storms (as in 8:5) ; these were apparently connected with some of the judgments involved in God's gaining possession of the earth. But the specific details are not revealed, a voice from heaven forbidding John to do so.

CONFIRMATION BY THE ANGEL, 10:5-7

The angel now confirms with an oath the purpose of God to take His rightful inheritance. He first takes the position of oath-taking (v. 5), raising his hand to heaven. The basis of his oath is God who is described here as the eternal One and as the all-powerful Creator (v. 6). The fact that the angel does not swear by himself may indicate that he is not Christ. The affirmation made in the oath is that the mystery of God will be finished soon. "There should be time no longer" presents some problem of interpretation. Many translations contain a marginal note indicating that the word "time" should be translated "delay." This is apparently allowable,* though this is an interpretative translation based on the content of verse 7. The idea is that there should no longer be an interval of time, that is, a delay, because (v. 7) the mystery of God will be finished when the seventh angel sounds.

> This expression, "the *mystery* of God," in this connection seems to indicate all those counsels and dealings of God made known by Him to and through the Old Testament prophets, concerning His governmental proceedings with men on earth looking always toward the establishment of the kingdom in the hands of Christ. When Christ comes to take the kingdom, there will be no mystery, but, on the contrary, manifestation.†

---

*W. F. Arndt and F. W. Gingrich (eds.), *A Greek-English Lexicon* (Chicago: University of Chicago Press, 1957), p. 896.
†William R. Newell, *The Book of the Revelation* (Chicago: Moody Press, 1935), p. 143.

COMMAND CONCERNING THE ANGEL, 10:8-10

SOURCE, V. 8

The voice spoke to John. This is the same voice that forbade him to write the content of the thunders in verse 4.

SUBSTANCE, V. 8

The voice commanded John to take the opened book from the angel's hand.

OBEDIENCE, VV. 9-10

When John asked the angel for the book, the angel told him to eat it and predicted that it would be bitter in his stomach, though sweet to his taste. John obeyed and found it so (v. 10).

OBJECT, VV. 9-10

What was the point of this? The opened book apparently contained revelations from God. It included some of the things which John was about to write in revealing them to us. Whether or not it contained all the remainder of the book of Revelation is of little consequence; it contained some of it at least. The point of this interlude during which John was commanded to assimilate these prophecies before he wrote them is simply that it is necessary for the prophet of God to let the Word of God affect him first before he ministers it to others.

This action is also a very vivid picture of the principle that although the fact of revelation may be pleasant to the taste, the contemplation or digestion of the truth may bring heaviness. This principle ought especially to be operative in our study of prophecy. Too often when one enters into an understanding of things to come he never gets beyond the tasting stage. But when one digests all of the truth of judgment to come it can only bring heaviness of heart to the child of God. While John "was doubtless delighted with the *fact* of a new revelation from the Lord, he nevertheless was distressed with the *nature* of that revelation. While he doubtless rejoiced in a measure at the revelation of the coming triumph and glory, yet he was saddened and grieved because preceding that glory were to occur the most terrible judgments and martyrdoms of all history."‡ As it was with John, so may it be with us.

COMMISSION OF THE ANGEL, 10:11

Finally, John is commissioned. The "he said" is literally "they say"—a plural of indefinite statement. Whether this commission came from the angel or the voice of some unnamed source is neither obvious nor important. The commission is that the prophet must (*dei,* it is necessary) prophesy again. Full of the sweet taste and bitterness of the little book, necessity was laid upon him to prophesy. He is to prophesy before many. The word "before" is *epi,* and it has several meanings. As Swete said:

> The Seer is not sent to prophesy in their presence (epi with gen., cf. Mc. xiii.9 . . .), nor against them (epi with acc. . . .), but simply with a view to their several cases. . . . It is no one Empire or Emperor that is concerned in the prophecies of the second half of the Apocalypse; not merely Rome or Nero or Domitian, but a multitude of races, kingdoms, and crowned heads.§

In other words, these prophecies concern many peoples, and this is the content of the little book.

‡J. B. Smith, *A Revelation of Jesus Christ* (Scottdale, Pa.: Herald Press, 1961), p. 162.
§Henry Barclay Swete, *The Apocalypse of St. John* (London: Macmillan, 1907), p. 132.

XI

THE TEMPLE, THE TWO WITNESSES
AND THE TRUMPET
11:1-19

THE TEMPLE, 11:1-2

OF THE ACTION of these verses John is no longer merely a witness. He is instructed to measure the sanctuary and for this purpose a reed is put into his hands. This reed was apparently a species of cane which grew in the Jordan valley to the height of fifteen to twenty feet. This one was straight like a rod though its length is not stated (Ezekiel's was six cubits or about nine feet, Ezek. 40:5). John was told to measure the temple (*naos,* the inner temple or the holy place and the holy of holies), the altar (probably the altar of incense which was in the holy place) and the worshipers. These worshipers will be the faithful, believing Jews of the tribulation days. This temple is the one which will be built in Jerusalem (cf. v. 8) during the tribulation and in which ancient Jewish rites will be reinstituted. It is apparently the same temple in which the man of sin will seat himself demanding to be worshiped and overthrowing the Jewish worship (II Thess. 2:4). The measuring itself seems to be an act of knowing, claiming or staking out. In this act of John, God is giving assurance that He will take note of those who faithfully worship Him in the tribulation days.

The outer court of the Gentiles is not measured. Instead
John is told to "cast it out" ("leave out," AV). The language
indicates utter rejection and the reason is given—the Gentiles
will tread underfoot the city of Jerusalem forty-two months.
This will occur during the last part of the tribulation when the
man of sin overthrows Jewish worship and establishes his own.
Thus the functioning worship of the temple described in
11:1-2*a* occurs during the first part of the tribulation, while
the treading down of the city by Gentiles (11:2*b*) follows during the last forty-two months.

Two important spiritual principles are exhibited in these
verses. First, God is cognizant of all that is going on; and
second, God sets the limits of persecution.

Two Witnesses, 11:3-14

TIME, V. 3

The time limit of the ministry of the two witnesses is stated
explicitly as 1,260 days. There is some disagreement over
whether this refers to the first or the last half of the tribulation. The text does not specify which. It seems to this author
that it refers to the first since it is the coming of the beast onto
the scene in power that terminates their witness (v. 7.) Although present and active during the first part of the tribulation chiefly as a political figure, he does not show himself in
his true character and demand to be worshiped until the middle of the tribulation. Therefore, it seems that he will cause
the death of the two witnesses who have been ministering
during the first part of the tribulation. If this be so, then, of
course, they will be witnessing along with the 144,000 during
this time.

TRAITS, 4-6

Their character, v. 4. These men are described as two olive
trees and two candlesticks. The figure of olive trees is brought
over from Zechariah 4:3, 14 and means that they are anointed

ones. The figure of the two candlesticks may also be from the same passage (where there is one lampstand), but it evidently refers to the witnesses' character as light bearers of the truth of God.

Their conduct, vv. 5-6. The conduct of their ministry is spectacular to say the least. They will have power (1) to kill their enemies with fire, (2) to keep it from raining, (3) to turn the waters to blood, and (4) to bring plagues upon the earth. The first two are reminiscent of Elijah and the last two of Moses.

TERMINATION, 7-10

Time, v. 7. Their ministry will be terminated only when "they shall have finished their testimony." They will be invincible until their work is done, and only then will God permit them to be killed.

Means, v. 7. The means of their death will be the rise of "the beast that ascendeth out of the bottomless pit." This is the first of thirty-six references to the beast in the book. Martyrdom of the witnesses will apparently be his first great act and will doubtless win him the support of many people.

Display, vv. 8-9. Their bodies will be put on public display in the streets of Jerusalem, which is identified as the city where the Lord was crucified and is characterized here as Sodom. Their bodies will be denied burial though the law allowed burial the same day even for the worst of criminals (Deut. 21:22-23). This action reflects the hardened spiritual condition of the people. Seiss says:

> The exposure of their dead bodies tells of a most extraordinary malignity and spite, and attests the extraordinary potency and effectiveness of the objects of it. It shows at once a devilishness of unwonted intensity in the people, and a terribleness of efficiency in the Witnesses in provoking a fiendishness and resentment so monstrous and unrelenting that it could not be placated by their death,

but continued to reek and vent itself upon their lifeless
remains after they were dead.°

Effect, v. 10. As if the display of their decaying bodies were
not enough, the people of the earth will make a holiday of
this occasion and send gifts to each other. This is the only
mention of rejoicing on the earth during the entire tribulation,
and it is over the death of the two witnesses. So overjoyed
are the people because their tormentors are dead that this becomes a happy holiday for them. Had they believed their
witness and received their message, the effect of their death
would have been received quite differently.

TRANSLATION, vv. 11-14

God intervenes. The two witnesses will be raised up after
three and a half days and will be translated into heaven in the
(not "an") cloud (of shekinah glory). Their restoration to life
and miraculous translation to heaven will strike fear in those
who see it. Perhaps for the moment they will realize that there
is a power greater than that of the beast. It is not difficult to
imagine the scene. A crowd will be standing around or filing
past their bodies lying in the street. Undoubtedly there will
be radio and television coverage. Suddenly they will stand up;
a voice (not the announcer's!) will be heard from heaven;
the two witnesses will disappear out of sight in the cloud of
glory.

Before the newspapers can report the story or the commentators write their interpretations there will be another great
event to cover, an earthquake centering in Jerusalem which
destroys a tenth part of the city and kills 7,000 men. "The
remnant" (v. 13) is literally "the rest." The word does not
necessarily indicate a spiritually saved group but simply the
rest of those living in Jerusalem who were not killed in the
earthquake. The remnant becomes terrified and gives glory

°J. A. Seiss, *The Apocalypse* (Grand Rapids: Zondervan Pub. House,
1865), II, 235-36.

to God. Some may be converted because of this experience, but some will simply recognize divine power without personal repentance.

This is the end of the second woe and brings the sounding of the seventh and last trumpet.

TRUMPET, 11:15-19

ANNOUNCEMENT, v. 15

The parenthetical portion between the sixth and seventh trumpets has now concluded (10:1—11:14). With the sounding of the seventh trumpet comes an announcement. Many texts read "the kingdom" instead of the plural. In either case the meaning is that the dominion of the world is taken over by Christ. Some additional events have to transpire before all is realized, but the end is near now and the announcement can be made. This will be the fulfillment of many Old Testament prophecies (Ps. 2:2; Dan. 2:44; Isa. 9:6-7).

ADORATION, vv. 16-17

The twenty-four elders on the thrones (not seats) fall down before God and worship Him for taking what is rightfully His.

ANGER, v. 18

This verse seems to be a continuation of the words of the elders. In the accomplishing of Christ taking the reins of government, nations will be angry, the wicked dead will be punished, and the righteous will be rewarded. The anger of the nations reaches a climax in 19:19. In other words, when Christ comes to reign, full justice will be meted out and all things will be set right.

ARK, v. 19

That there is a temple of God in heaven is not surprising since the tabernacle was constructed after a pattern of things in the heavens (Heb. 9:23). But the worship of God on the earth in the tribulation temple has been defiled by the beast. In the heavenly temple the ark is seen at this point shining through, as it were, the lightnings, voices, thunderings, earthquake and hail. The ark was the place of the presence of God and the reminder of the faithfulness of God. Here, just before the outpouring of final judgment, is a reminder of God's faithfulness to His own people.

ADDITIONAL NOTE ON THE IDENTIFICATION OF THE TWO WITNESSES

Through the years many have attempted to identify the two witnesses. This much is certain: (1) They are persons, for all the other times that the word "witness" is used in the New Testament it is used of persons. They are not movements or powers, but individual persons. (2) It is also certain that they are not named in the text, and this writer feels that the case should be left there. These are two exceptional witnesses raised up by God during the tribulation and preserved by Him until their ministry is completed.

Nevertheless, there have been many attempts at identification.

Elijah. Similarity is noted between his ministry (James 5: 17; II Kings 1:10-12), his manner of being taken to heaven (II Kings 2:11), and the fact that Elijah must come before the day of the Lord (Mal. 4:5; Matt. 17:10-11).

Moses. Similarity is noted between his ministry and that of the witnesses (water turned to blood, Exodus 7:20), and his presence on the Mount of Transfiguration with Elijah sets him apart as an important witness.

Enoch. Since Enoch and Elijah were the only two persons to be translated without seeing death, it is argued that they will be the two witnesses, since all men must die (Heb. 9:27). But what about all those saints who will be translated in the rapture? Also, Enoch's day in which he prophesied was an evil one like the tribulation.

XII

WAR

12:1-17

CHAPTER 12 is a description of war—first on the earth (vv. 1-6), then in heaven (vv. 7-12), and finally back on the earth (vv. 13-17). It not only reveals future things, but it also unveils the sphere of Satan and angels.

WAR ON EARTH—PHASE I, 12:1-6

TWO WONDERS, vv. 1-4a

We are first introduced to two wonders or literally, "signs." "Sign" (*semeion*) is used seven times in the book (12:1, 3; 13:13-14; 15:1; 16:14; 19:29) to indicate an object with a special meaning. The first sign is a woman (vv. 1-2). This is the second of four women mentioned in the book (Jezebel, 2:20; the harlot, 17:4; the bride, 19:7). The description of this woman is reminiscent of Genesis 37:9-10. The obvious impression conveyed by the description is one of great splendor. The woman is crowned and is arrayed in great glory. The use of sun, moon and stars is not to identify her but to describe her. Who she is must be determined from another consideration, namely, her relation to the child. Since the child is clearly Christ (from the description of His ruling in v. 5 compared with Ps. 2:9; Rev. 2:27; 19:15), the woman must be the one who bore Christ—Israel. That she is Israel and not only Mary

77

is corroborated by the fact that it is this woman who is persecuted during the last half of the tribulation (vv. 13 ff.) . The
woman is further described as being in travail at the birth of
Christ. The picture is a paradox—a queenly woman in suffering.

The second sign is a dragon (vv. 3-4a) . The identification
of this sign is made in verse 9. The dragon is Satan, but his
description in these verses is startling. The use of a dragon to
picture Satan itself indicates his intense cruelty. The adjective
"red" indicates his murderous, bloodthirsty character. The
seven heads and ten horns relate him to the beast (13:1) and
the diadems on his heads show his regal power. With his tail
he is said to draw a third part of the stars of heaven and cast
(aorist tense, indicating a definite event) them to earth. The
problem is, what are the stars? They could be the luminous
bodies seen in the heavens, in which case this event would be
some sort of judgment involving a meteor shower on the earth.
But sometimes stars refer to angelic beings (as 9:1; Job 38:7;
and possibly Rev. 1:20) . If that is the reference here, then the
event described is the revolt of Satan in which he took with
him in rebellion a third of the angels (cf. Jude 6; II Peter 2:4) .

THE WAR, 4b-6

Verse 4 is actually two sentences, and a period should be
placed where the Authorized Version has a colon. Verse 4b
goes back to the time of the birth of Christ and Satan's efforts
to destroy Him (Matt. 2:13) . Christ's birth is stated in verse
5; He is identified as the ultimate Ruler of the nations; then
His ascension is mentioned, passing by His entire life and His
passion. The reason for this omission is simply that the point
of the passage is Satan's war against Christ. Satan failed to
destroy Him at His birth and the fact that He ascended proves
that he failed to destroy Him during His life and even in His
death. The ascension is the proof of Satan's failure. What is
the relation of verse 6 to the story? Since Satan failed to kill

Christ, he turns his attention to the woman, Israel, to pour out his vengeance on her. The details of the persecution for three and a half years are recorded in verses 13-17.

WAR IN HEAVEN, 12:7-12

OPPONENTS, v. 7

The scene shifts to heaven and to a war between Michael and his angels and Satan and his angels. Michael means "who is like God," and he is the only angel called specifically an archangel in the Scriptures (Jude 9; cf. Dan. 10:13, 21; 12:1). In Jude 9 there is recorded a conflict between the two leaders, Michael and Satan. Here the war is between them and their armies.

OUTCOME, vv. 8-12

In relation to the earth, vv. 8-9, 12b. The result of the battle is defeat for Satan and his hosts. They are cast out of heaven and into the earth. In verse 9 Satan has five titles. "Dragon" indicates his fierce nature, "serpent" his crafty character. "Devil" means accuser or slanderer and "Satan" means adversary. He is also called "the deceiver of the whole world." In verse 12 the voice from heaven announces woe on the inhabitants of the earth because the devil has been barred from heaven and will wage his total warfare on the earth. There are two reasons for this woe in verse 12: (1) because of Satan's confinement to the earth as his only sphere of operation, and (2) because he knows he does not have much more time before his final defeat and total confinement.

In relation to heaven, vv. 10-12a. At this defeat of Satan (which probably occurs at the middle point of the tribulation) a voice in heaven breaks into praise. It announces salvation and the kingdom since one more major conquest has been made in the march toward inevitable victory for Christ. Something is revealed about Satan's work through the years of history and the means of victory over him (vv. 10-11). He is labeled "the accuser of our brethren." H. A. Ironside used to say, "Satan is the accuser of the brethren; let's leave the dirty work to him!" His activity continues day and night and it is before God (thus making it clear that this has been and is his work up to the middle of the tribulation when he will be cast out from heaven).

But there is a way of victory over Satan, and this is revealed in verse 11. "They" refers to the brethren of verse 10. There are three elements in the formula for victory in verse 11. (1) The basis is the blood of the Lamb. Blood is the evidence of death; thus the death of Christ is the basis for all victory over Satan. (2) The activity that overcomes Satan is testimony or witness. Even if it leads to death (as it does), the witness will be effective in defeating Satan. (3) The attitude involved in victory is complete self-sacrifice even to the point of being willing to die. All the inexplicable persecutions, tortures and martyrdoms of saints in all ages are made right by this verse. Seeming defeat is ultimate victory over the enemy of our souls.

War on Earth—Phase II, 12:13-17

ANTAGONISTS, v. 13

As anticipated in verse 6, Satan's attack after his being cast out of heaven centers on the woman, Israel.

ASYLUM, v. 14

Eagles' wings indicate rapid flight which will be necessary for Israel to escape the attacks of the dragon through his agents (cf. Matt. 24:16 for the flight and Exodus 19:4; Deut. 32:11-12 for eagles' wings). Apparently these fleeing people will find asylum in some place in the wilderness which will give them a certain amount of natural protection for time, times, and half a time, or three and one-half years (the last part of the tribulation). Some have thought this wilderness refuge will be the presently deserted city of Petra in southern Palestine.

ATTACK, vv. 15-17

Satan (who can cause miracles to happen too) will launch his attack with a flood, apparently in order to try to drown people out of their wilderness refuge. God in turn will cause something to make the earth open (an earthquake?) in order to consume the water of the flood and thus save the persecuted people. When he fails to conquer or destroy those who have fled to the wilderness, Satan turns his attack on "the remnant of her seed." The word "remnant" is *loipoi* which elsewhere in Revelation applies to groups of individuals in a general sense and not necessarily a spiritual remnant. Indeed, the words for the faithful in Israel are different in Romans 9:27 and 11:5. These are the rest who did not flee. All of those whom Satan will attack are the remnant in the sense of being on God's side; otherwise he would not be interested in attacking them. Some flee into the wilderness asylum; the rest do not, and it is upon them that Satan unleashes his attack in verse 17.

XIII

THE BEAST AND HIS PROPHET
13:1-18

THE BEAST, 13:1-10

APPEARANCE, VV. 1 2

THIS BEAST has already been introduced (11:7) but now there is given a complete description of his person and work. In the vision he arose out of the sea which many understand to be a symbol of the masses of people (17:15). Perhaps his origin out of the sea simply distinguishes him in the vision from the second beast who arises out of the land. The beast has seven heads, ten horns, crowns on the horns, and the names of blasphemy on his heads. The beast is a kingdom, for the ten horns are identified as ten kings in 17:12; yet they are united in one beast. In other words, he represents a confederation of ten. The seven heads are also explained in 17:9 as the seven hills of the city in which his power centers (Rome). They also stand for seven Roman rulers of which he is the last. Therefore, the beast is not only a kingdom but also an individual ruler. He is a man. This is known from II Thessalonians 2 where he as an individual—not a kingdom—sits in the temple as God. This is why his heads are covered with names (the plural is correct) of blasphemy. Roman emperors in the past blasphemed by designating themselves as God. This man will do the same (II Thess. 2:4).

In total appearance the beast was *like* a leopard, his feet *like* those of a bear and his mouth *like* a lion's. In the vision of Daniel 7 the first beast that the prophet saw was like a lion, the second like a bear, and the third like a leopard. John's beast combines these features; whatever the Babylonian, Medo-Persian and Grecian empires had of strength, brutality and swiftness will be present in this final form of world rule in the western confederation of nations (or, as it is sometimes called, the revived Roman Empire).

Great as this man and empire will be, he is actually only an agent or tool of someone else. It is the dragon or Satan who gives the beast his power, his throne (not seat) and authority. He is sold out to Satan, and Satan uses him to the fullest.

ACCLAIM, VV. 3-4

Cause v. 3. One of the heads of the beast was "wounded to death." Literally it reads, "as having been slain to death." This is exactly the same word that was used in 5:6 of the Lamb where it was translated "as it had been slain." If Christ died actually, then it appears that this ruler will also actually die. But his wound will be healed, which can only mean restoration to life. In 11:7 he was seen as coming out of the abyss, and that coincides with his restoration to life here. He apparently actually dies, descends to the abyss and returns to life. The world understandably wonders after him.

Character, v. 4. The world will worship the beast. The "all" of verse 3 is qualified by verse 8. Those whose names are written in the book of life will not worship him, but all others will. Worship means acknowledgment of worth, and the worth which people acknowledge in the beast is twofold: his uniqueness ("Who is like unto the beast?") , and his might ("Who is able to make war with him?") .

ACTIVITY, VV. 5-7*a.*

His activity includes blasphemy and war. Notice that the

former is a religious activity and the latter a political one. He is not only a political ruler, but he seeks to exert religious domination too. His mouth speaks great things and blasphemies against God (cf. Dan. 7:25). He will blaspheme the name of God, the dwelling place of God (His tabernacle) and those who dwell in heaven (the saints who will already be there).

Further, the beast will be allowed ("it was given," v. 7) to make war with the saints (cf. 12:17). "Overcome" indicates that he will kill them. All of this activity, however, is directly under the control of God. His ability to make war is permitted by God, and all of his power is limited to forty-two months (v. 5). Here is an example of the interweaving of the forces that go to make up events—God controls all, yet Satan controls the beast who in turn acts on his own in blaspheming. Men who compose his army will serve him voluntarily to make martyrs of God's people who, though they give up their lives, are still within God's protecting care!

AUTHORITY, vv. 7b-10

Extent, vv. 7b-8. The beast's authority extends to all peoples except those whose names are in the book of life. The word "people" should be added after kindreds in verse 7. The phrase "book of life" occurs seven times in Revelation (3:5; 13:8; 17:8; 20:12, 15; 21:27; 22:19) and only one time elsewhere in the New Testament (Phil. 4:3).

End, vv. 9-10. The phrasing of verse 9 indicates a call to serious attention. An important principle is about to be announced in verse 10. It is the principle of retribution. After all that has been said about the power of the beast, verse 10 is a word of great comfort. The captor will be taken captive; the killer will be killed. When God's purposes are finished through the beast, God will take him captive and confine him to the lake of fire. In the knowledge of this is the patience and faith that sustains the saints who endure these persecutions.

THE FALSE PROPHET, 13:11-18

APPEARANCE, V. 11

This second beast arises from the earth and is thereby distinguished from the first one who came from the sea in the vision. His appearance also is different—less pretentious. He has two horns (instead of ten) like a lamb. The horns suggest strength, though less strength than the first beast, and the lamb may allude to an appearance of meekness or innocence and may also indicate his character as an imitation of the Lamb of God. This beast is no weak person, however, for he speaks as a dragon.

AIM, V. 12

The aim of this second person is to promote the worship of the first beast. At no time in his career does he promote himself, but his interests are always concerned with the first beast. Verse 12 declares that his power is as great as that of the first beast but he uses it in the interests of the first beast.

ACTIVITY, VV. 13-17

In order to accomplish his aim, this second beast will be empowered to do certain things.

Fire on earth. He will make fire come down on the earth in duplication of the power of the two witnesses to show the world that he has as much power as they had (v. 13).

Other miracles. He will perform other miracles (literally, signs in vv. 13-14).

Image of first beast. He will order the earth dwellers to make an image of the first beast (v. 14) and from what follows we understand that they do it willingly and quickly, for his next step is to give life to that image which they will make. The word for life is *pneuma* (spirit). This could indicate a supernatural miracle (performed by the power of Satan) which actually gives life to the image. Or, the word may be translated "wind" and indicate some magical sleight of hand which the second beast performs that gives the appearance of real life to this image. The speech and movements of the image could easily be manufactured.

Identification with beast. He will force men to become identified with the beast by a mark which they must receive in their foreheads or hands. The word "mark" means an impress made by a stamp, like a brand used on slaves and animals. Men will become slaves of the beast and have the identifying mark of their slavery. Without it they cannot buy or sell.

What will this mark be like? Verse 17 indicates that it will be either the name of the beast or his number. The second "or" in verse 17 should be omitted, making the phrase "the name of the beast or the number of his name" an appositive phrase explaining the mark. The number is further explained in verse 18 as 666. This is the number of the first beast, which number will be one of the options for the mark. In that coming day it will also be a means of identifying the beast to those who constitute the godly remnant.

So many identifications have been made of 666 with characters of history as to make them all unreliable coincidences. When this man arises on the scene of world affairs there will be no mistake as to who he is and in some way, unknown now, the number 666 will play a principal part in the identification. The mark is of the first beast, however, for he is the chief character in this chapter and the one whose worship is promoted by the second beast. For this reason the second beast is called elsewhere the false prophet; he is a prophet of the first beast (16:13; 19:20; 20:10).

ADDITIONAL NOTE ON THE TITLE "ANTICHRIST"

The term "antichrist" is a biblical one (I John 2:18, 22; 4:3; II John 7). It is used both of false teachers in John's day (and by example it may be used of false teachers in any day) and of the coming antichrist. In other words, the word is properly used in the present and future and in the singular and plural. Which of these beasts is the antichrist? The meaning of the word will not determine the answer, for both beasts are antichrists in the sense of being against Christ. Some feel that the second beast is the antichrist because he has to do chiefly with religious matters, while the first beast is principally concerned with political activities. The first beast is obviously a religious leader, however, for it is he who will be worshiped. Sometimes Daniel 11:37 is cited as showing that the antichrist will be a Jew and the reference is linked with the fact that the second beast comes from the land (symbolizing Israel). However, Daniel 11:37 might be translated "gods" as well as "God." It seems to this writer that the label "antichrist" is to be used with the more important personage, and that, of course, is the first beast. First John 2:18 indicates that there is coming one great antichrist. The Lord predicted that there would be many false prophets and many who claim to be Christ during the tribulation days (Matt. 24:11, 23). The title "antichrist," therefore, ought to be applied to the outstanding person among all these false people, and that is the first beast. Also, to this writer the first beast (whether you call him antichrist or not) is the man of sin (II Thess. 2:3), the little horn (Dan. 7:8), the prince that shall come (Dan. 9:26), the willful king (Dan. 11:36), and the beast (Rev. 11:7; 14:9, 11; 15:2; 16:2, 10, 13; 17:3-17; 19:19-20; 20:4, 10).

XIV

VARIOUS ANNOUNCEMENTS
14:1-20

SITUATION, V. 1

THE 144,000, 14:1-5

THE VISION OPENS with John seeing the (not "a") Lamb and 144,000 on Mount Zion. Some understand this to be anticipatory of the millennial state making Zion mean the earthly Jerusalem as it often does (II Sam. 5:7; Isa. 2:3). But since Zion is used of the heavenly Jerusalem (Heb. 12:22) and since these 144,000 are before the throne (v. 3) it seems more natural to understand Zion as the heavenly city. The important point, however, is that the 144,000 are now with the Lamb. When the group was first introduced they were on earth (7:1-3), but now they are in heaven. Their work of witnessing must now be finished, for none will be able to slay them until that is so. That they are the same group as in chapter 7 seems clear from (1) the fact that the distinctive number is exactly the same, and (2) that the seal of the name of God (literally in v. 1, "having his name and his Father's") in their foreheads is the same.

SONG, VV. 2-3

John next heard a great sound—like the voice of many waters (indicating the volume) and the sound of thunder (indicating its loudness). It resolved itself into the voice of harpers playing on harps and singing a new song. Verse 2 apparently speaks of the same group as verse 3, that is, the 144,000. Notice too that the 144,000 are distinct from the elders and the living ones. This proves that the 144,000 cannot be the same group as those represented by the elders.

SEPARATION, V. 4

Two things are said about their separation unto God. First, they are virgins. Although this could be understood to mean that these people were never married, it also can mean that they were completely separated unto the God they served. The word "virgin" is used this way of married Corinthian believers in II Corinthians 11:2. It includes men in that passage, Matthew 25:1 and here. Second, they followed Christ "whithersoever he goeth" including obedience unto death.

SALVATION, V. 4c

They are redeemed people who are said also to be firstfruits. From the Old Testament use of "firstfruits" this means that they are a token offering to God, which indicates that a larger harvest would follow. The first converts of a country are called firstfruits of the larger number to be won (Rom. 16:5; I Cor. 16:15). Christ is the firstfruits of the resurrection harvest (I Cor. 15:20, 23). Of what group are these 144,000 the firstfruits? Apparently they indicate the harvest of many other Israelites (remember that they are Jews, not Gentiles) who will turn to the Lord at the end of the tribulation and during the millennium (Isa. 2:3; Zech. 8:22).

SANCTIFICATION, V. 5

In some texts of verse 5 the word "lie" replaces the word "guile," and in certain texts the last phrase "before the throne of God" is omitted. Nevertheless, the verse describes the ultimate sanctification of these people.

EVERLASTING GOSPEL, 14:6-8

ANNOUNCEMENT, V. 6

An angel appears with the announcement of the (literally, "an") everlasting gospel. (See Gal. 1:8, though God does not use angels today to proclaim the gospel.)

INCLUSIVENESS, V. 6

The message of this gospel is to all the world. It is God's last call of grace to a world that persists in rejecting Him and that openly defies Him.

MESSAGE, V. 7

Its message is threefold: fear, glorify and worship God. The particular aspect of God's revelation of Himself in this instance is as *Creator*. If a man heeds this message, he will have to refuse to receive the mark of the beast, which will show as clearly as possible a heart change. In those days people will not risk their lives at the hands of the beast for a mere outward profession of salvation.

DOOM OF BABYLON, 14:8

This chapter is something like a table of contents of the things in the remainder of the book. Another angel now announces the fall of Babylon, which fall is described in detail in chapters 17 and 18.

CERTAINTY

The repetition of "is fallen" emphasizes the certainty of the utter destruction of Babylon. This is anticipatory since Babylon's actual fall is connected with the outpouring of the seventh vial (16:19).

CAUSE

The reason for Babylon's judgment is twofold: because of her own fornication and because she has infected all the nations with her sins.

DOOM OF BEAST WORSHIPERS, 14:9-13

PEOPLE, V. 9

The third angel announces judgment on all who worship the beast and his image and receive his mark. Notice that the mark may be placed in the forehead where all can see or in the hand where it could be hidden temporarily. *but God knows*

PUNISHMENT, VV. 10-11

The punishment is described in as terrible terms as occur elsewhere in the Bible. Its intensity is unmixed—literally "he shall drink of the wine of the anger of God mixed undiluted in the cup of his wrath." Its agents are fire and brimstone or sulphur. It will be a spectacle before the holy angels and the Lamb whom these people rejected. Its extent is forever (v. 11). Its character is continuous ("no rest day nor night," v. 11).

PATIENCE, VV. 12-13

In spite of the intensity of the beast's endeavors to bring all the world under his control, there will be some who will not yield but who will keep the commandments of God. In the midst of their persecution by the beast they will be helped to endure by remembering that ultimately the beast and all his followers will have to endure the eternal punishment described in verses 10-11. This verse is similar to 13:10b. A further announcement is made concerning these whom the beast will martyr in verse 13. They are called blessed. "From henceforth" indicates that this belongs particularly to those who will suffer under the beast. Their works in standing for the truth follow with them into heaven.

HARVEST OF THE EARTH, 14:14-20

REAPERS, VV. 14-18

The reapers of the harvest are the Lord (vv. 14, 16) and angles (v. 17). The Lord is pictured with a golden crown (*stephanos*, a victor's crown, not a diadem, indicating His coming as Conqueror) and a sharp sickle (to do the work of judging). An angel (v. 15) from the temple delivers the command from God to proceed with the harvest, and another angel (v. 17), also from the presence of God, appears with a sharp sickle to help in the harvesting (cf. Matt. 13:39).

REASON, VV. 15, 18

Within this section two figures are used, the harvest (vv. 14-16) and the vine (vv. 17-19). The harvest is said to be ripe (v. 15) and the grapes of the vine are also said to be ripe (v. 18). The two words are different, however. The ripe harvest is literally a dried or withered harvest (cf. Matt. 21:19-20; Mark 3:1, 3; John 15:6; Rev. 16:12). In other words, the inhabitants of the earth are withered, lifeless and fully ready for judgment. The grapes of the vine are also said to be ripe. This is the vine of the earth and stands in contrast to Christ, the true vine (Ps. 80:8; John 15:1). The picture here is that all the false religion of man is fully ripe and ready for harvest. Thus the harvest is ready because man in his own efforts apart from the life of God has fully developed an apostate religious system.

RESULT, VV. 19-20

If verses 14-16 picture the harvest of Matthew 13:36 ff., then of course there will be some who will be taken into kingdom blessing while others go into judgment. But the harvest of the grapes results only in judgment in the winepress of the wrath of God. In verse 20 this judgment is specified not as hell but as something that occurs on the earth ("trodden without the city"—Jerusalem). It apparently is a reference to the war of Armageddon (cf. 19:17-19) when the blood from the slaughter will flow 1,600 furlongs or 175 miles to the depth of the horses' bridles (or about four and a half feet). The valley of Megiddo where the war will be fought in the north of Palestine drains into the Jordan system, allowing sufficient mileage to fulfill literally this prediction.

XV

PRELUDE TO THE LAST JUDGMENTS

15:1-8

PLAGUES, 15:1

As WITH THE TRUMPET JUDGMENTS, angels are employed in the execution of these seven last plagues. These are the last, and when the seventh is poured out a voice cries, "It is done" (16: 17). "Filled up" should be translated "finished," and "wrath" is literally "anger." The outpouring of these plagues is described in chapter 16.

PERSONS, 15:2-4

IDENTITY, v. 2

John saw as it were a sea of glass mingled with fire. Such a sea appeared in the vision in 4:6 but here is mingled with fire, perhaps referring to the fiery persecution which these people had suffered under the beast. The group is clearly identified as those who had gotten victory over the beast although it cost them their lives. Undoubtedly the beast will think he gains the victory over these enemies whom he kills, but God says that they get victory over him (cf. 12:11). They have harps like the twenty-four elders (5:8) and the 144,000 (14:3).

ACTIVITY, vv. 3-4

They sing the song of Moses and the Lamb, ascribing praise to God for His mighty acts (cf. Exodus 15 and Deut. 32). The word "song" is repeated before the Lamb, so that they sing two songs—the song of Moses and the song of the Lamb (could this be Ps. 22?). The substance of both songs is the mighty works of God. To Him are ascribed several things. (1) He is almighty (cf. 1:8). (2) He is righteous and true. This attribute is particularly relevant in relation to the outpouring of these judgments. (3) He is the King of nations (not "saints" as in the AV). This kingship is about to be exercised, for the setting up of the kingdom on the earth is imminent. (4) He is holy and for this reason men should fear and glorify Him (cf. 14:7). (5) He will be worshiped by the nations, again referring to the time of the establishment of the kingdom. This is the One whose wrath is about to be poured out in these seven last plagues.

PREPARATION, 15:5-8

A new vision opens which involves the commissioning of the outpouring of these plagues. It is a vision of the temple in heaven and particularly of the "tabernacle of the testimony," that is, the holy place. It is opened to reveal seven angels coming out. This emphasizes the fact that the judgments of God are not vindictive but vindicative, coming out of the sanctuary itself. To these angels comes one of the four living ones with seven golden vials of these last judgments. The word "vial" is better translated "bowl," like an incense bowl (cf. 5:8 for the same word). These contain the wrath of God, and until they are poured out no one can enter the temple because of the smoke (probably a symbol of the judgment connected with these plagues as in Exodus 19:18; Isaiah 6:4). Certainly the smoke adds to the total picture of the terror of these imminent judgments.

XVI

THE SEVEN BOWL JUDGMENTS
16:1-21

UNLIKE THE PREVIOUS SERIES of judgments of the trumpets and
seals, each of which had a break between the sixth and seventh
judgments, the seven plagues of the bowls are poured out without interruption and apparently quite rapidly. All of the angels receive their orders to go at the same time (v. 1), which
would indicate that these judgments follow each other in quick
succession (vv. 13-16, however, seem to be a parenthetical excursus).

FIRST BOWL, 16:2

The first plague is upon the earth and results in a grievous
sore. It is described as "bad and evil." Swete believes this
means bad and actively evil, that is, malignant in the technical
sense.* The extent of this affliction is limited to those who
are followers of the beast, the believing remnant being exempt (cf. Exodus 9:8-12). Apparently the beast cannot heal
them, for they are still cursing God for these sores after the
fifth bowl has been poured out (v. 11). Notice too that the
beast is in power and his image has been set up when this first
bowl judgment comes. It would seem therefore that this series
of judgments occurs at the close of the tribulation period.

*Henry Barclay Swete, *The Apocalypse of St. John* (London: Macmillan, 1907), p. 201.

96

SECOND BOWL, 16:3

The second bowl is poured on the sea, with the result that the waters become blood and every living thing in the sea dies. The "as" is misplaced in the Authorized Version, the correct reading being "became blood as of a dead man." The vivid image is of a dead person wallowing in his own blood. The seas will wallow in blood. Under the second trumpet, one-third of the sea creatures died (8:9); now the destruction is complete. The stench and disease that this will cause along the shores of the seas of the earth are unimaginable.

THIRD BOWL, 16:3-7

The third plague follows the pattern of the third trumpet and affects the fresh water supply so that it becomes blood. The victims of this judgment will experience the inexorable law of retribution. They shed the blood of the saints and prophets, so they must now drink blood. "They are worthy" (v. 6) refers to the victims of this judgment. They deserve what they receive. Another angel from the altar echoes the refrain of the righteousnesss of God's judgments. The only reason it is difficult for people to conceive of God dealing in this manner is that for thousands of years He has been long-suffering and gracious, not meting out the judgment which the world deserved.

FOURTH BOWL, 16:8-9

The fourth judgment affects the sun so that "power was given unto him" (the sun) to scorch men. Instead of turning to God and pleading for mercy, men blaspheme His name and do not repent.

FIFTH BOWL, 16:10-11

The fifth plague is on the throne of the beast and brings darkness to the seat of his government. Undoubtedly this slows up his attempt to force all men to worship him or be killed.

The beast will not have enough time to be able to enforce his edict universally. The result of this plague is that men gnaw their tongues and blaspheme God for their pains and sores (which they received under the previous judgments and which are still with them).

SIXTH BOWL, 16:12-16

The sixth judgment will dry up the Euphrates River (which previously had been turned to blood). This is done to facilitate the crossing of the armies of the kings of the east (cf. Dan. 11:44) as they rush to the final war of Armageddon. This is an actual drying up of the river which forms the eastern border of Palestine (Gen. 15:18). The mention of the kings of the east introduces an excursus on Armageddon (vv. 13-16).

John saw three unclean spirits like frogs come out of the mouths of the trinity of evil—the dragon (Satan), the beast (13:1-10) and the false prophet (13:11-18). They are identified as demons (v. 14) and their task is to woo the kings of the earth to the war of Armageddon. The word means "hill of Megiddo" and is located on the southern rim of the plain of Esdraelon where the war (series of battles) will take place. God is directing this (v. 16); demons accomplish it (v. 19); Satan, the beast and the false prophet are involved in it (v. 13); yet the kings of the earth will come together without any sense of compulsion (Dan. 11:44). How intricate are the ways of God!

In the midst of this rehearsal concerning Armageddon comes a warning and appeal for purity and watchfulness (v. 15). Grace is still offered even in the face of persistent and shameless rejection.

SEVENTH BOWL, 16:17-21

The last judgment brings widespread destruction and havoc. With it comes the cry "It is done." This is accompanied by physical signs and disturbances. The earthquake divides "the great city"—Jerusalem, and causes other cities to fall. Babylon is fully judged (details are in chaps. 17-18), islands and mountains disappear, and a great hail falls, each stone weighing about one hundred twenty-five pounds. Yet, in spite of the severity and universality of these last judgments, some men will survive and—unbelievable as it is—will persist in blaspheming God rather than turning to Him for mercy. Everything that man has built will crumble before his eyes. Quite literally the whole world will collapse around him, yet he will persist in thinking he is still the master of his own fate without any need for God.

The conclusion of this series of judgments brings us to the second coming of Chirst. This is described in chapter 19, but John is first given a vision of the details concerning Babylon which has been mentioned several times before.

XVII
RELIGIOUS BABYLON
17:1-18

THE DESTRUCTION OF BABYLON which has already been referred
to in the book (14:8; 16:19) is described in detail in chapters
17 and 18. The emphasis in chapter 17 is on the religious and
political aspects of Babylon and in 18 on the commercial aspect. Babylon is both a city and a system. It had its beginnings
with the building of the tower of Babel (Gen. 10:10) and it
flourished under Nebuchadnezzar. Whether the city will be
rebuilt once again on the Euphrates is a matter of debate (cf.
Isa. 13:19-20; 21:9; Jer. 50—51). Nevertheless, the name is
used for more than a city in these chapters; it also stands for
a system. This is much the same as the way Americans speak
of Wall Street or Madison Avenue. They are actual streets,
but they also stand for the financial or advertising enterprises.
Babylon is used in a similar sense in these chapters standing
for a religious and political system in chapter 17 and a commercial empire in chapter 18.

DESCRIPTION OF BABYLON, 17:1-7

AGENT, v. 1

It was one of the bowl angels who revealed these details to
John. The words "Come hither" occur again in 21:9.

DETAILS, VV. 1-6

Harlot, vv. 1-2. Four times this characteristic of the false religious system of the tribulation days is mentioned in this chapter (vv. 1, 5, 15-16; cf. 19:2). This church is unfaithful to the Lord and thus is a harlot. When believers are taken to heaven in the rapture before the tribulation begins, religion does not disappear from the earth. Indeed, it will flourish under this unfaithful Babylon for the first part of the tribulation until destroyed by the beast. Tribulation saints, of course, will be outside this false church. The harlotry of this system will extend to "many waters," which means to many people (v. 15) and will include alliances with kings of the earth. In other words, the power of this church will be enhanced by political alliances.

Political power, v. 3. John next saw the woman sitting on the beast. The beast is clearly seen to be the man of sin of 13:1-10 by comparing the description in verse 3 with 13:1. The startling feature of this scene is that the whore is sitting on the beast, indicating that she will have power over the man of sin. This event must occur during the first part of the tribulation before the man of sin overthrows religion and requires everyone to worship him.

Glory, v. 4. The harlot is bedecked with splendor signifying her glory and wealth.

Counterfeit, v. 5a. Her name is called a mystery. (Note that the word "mystery" is not an adjective—"mystery Babylon"—but a noun in apposition with Babylon—"mystery, Babylon.") The Christian will realize by the use of this word "mystery" that this Babylon is not the city on the Euphrates but a secret use of the word (explained in 17:9, 18). Since the true church is also called a mystery (Eph. 5:32), this apostate church is a counterfeit.

Federation, 5b. The harlot is also the mother of harlots. In other words, many groups will join together under the one harlot in a kind of federated church. With the identification in 17:9 and with the interrelation of Babylon and practices of the Roman Catholic Church, it is difficult to escape the conclusion that the Roman church is the harlot. But this is not the whole picture, for the apostate church is not merely the Roman Church. It will include other groups in a family relationship with their mother. The tie that will bind them together will be their harlotry.

Persecutor, v. 6. The church will be a persecutor of the believers in Jesus during this time, and she will be successful. "Admiration" in verse 6 should be translated "wonder."

PROMISE, V. 7

The entire vision seems to have been enigmatic to John. The angel asks him, "Why didst thou wonder?" So the angel promises John an explanation of the matters which he had seen.

MATTERS WHICH CONCERN BABYLON, 17:8-15

BEAST, V. 8

The beast is identified first. He is the same one referred to in 11:7 as coming from the abyss. Here it is said that he "is about to come up," indicating that the events of verses 1-7 precede his rise to power in the middle of the tribulation period.

HEADS, VV. 9-11

First, the seven heads of the beast are identified as the seven mountains on which the harlot sits. "No reasonable doubt can be entertained as to the meaning of these words. The Seven hills of Rome were a commonplace with the Latin poets."* In other words, the center of the beast's power is Rome.

---

*Henry Barclay Swete, *The Apocalypse of St. John* (London: Macmillan, 1907), p. 220.

As to the identification of the kings (v. 10), there is greater difficulty. They apparently have something to do with Rome, and some have interpreted them as a selective list of Roman emperors (since more than five had reigned until John's time). Others have suggested that they refer to successive forms of government in the Roman Empire. Objections can be raised to both of these views, and the matter cannot be settled with certainty. In any case, the beast that is to come during the tribulation is definitely said to be the eighth (v. 11), and his power is limited and his doom certain.

HORNS, vv. 12-14

The horns of the beast are ten kings (Dan. 7:23-24). These are the ten nations who are allowed to rule for one hour. That expression should be understood as meaning one purpose or activity (cf. Luke 22:53). To suit the beast's own purpose they are allowed to rule as independent entities. But this independence is only on the surface. They will give their power to the beast (v. 13), and together make war with the Lamb. Daniel reveals that three of these ten nations will evidently rebel so that the beast has to take them over forcibly (7:24). Of course, they cannot defeat the Lamb so they are overcome. Christ's titles, "King of kings" and "Lord of lords," are especially significant in light of the lordship the beast will assume over these kings.

WATERS, v. 15

The waters on which the harlot sits (v. 1) are now explained as the peoples of the world. The apostate church will be ecumenical.

DESTRUCTION OF BABYLON, 17:16-18

Religious Babylon who sought political alliances and power will in the end be destroyed by a political alliance. It will be these ten nations who "make her desolate." The words "deso-

late," "naked," "eat," and "burn" all show the completeness
of her annihilation. In verse 17 is found another example of
the interweaving of the purposes of God with the desires of
men. The kings will voluntarily join forces to destroy the
harlot, but in so doing they are in reality fulfilling the purpose
of God. It is God who will incline them to align themselves
with the beast until, literally, "the words of God are finished
or accomplished." Finally, the identification of the woman is
further pinned down to the city previously mentioned (v. 9),
that is, Rome. This makes it impossible to disassociate apostate Christendom of the tribulation days from Rome. Rome
will be the religious and political center of the world in the
tribulation.

To summarize this chapter: Religion will flourish during
the first part of the tribulation in the false system called Babylon, the harlot. This system centers in Rome, includes other
harlot groups, and exercises great political influence. For the
first half of the tribulation she will reign unchallenged; but at
the middle of the tribulation, the beast (the man of sin) will
see her as a challenge to his own power and program. So with
his league of ten nations he will destroy the harlot and set
himself up to be worshiped.

XVIII

COMMERCIAL BABYLON

18:1-24

BABYLON INVOLVES A CITY (certainly Rome and perhaps Babylon on the Euphrates) and a system. The religious aspect of that system was described in the preceding chapter; this chapter concerns other facets of Babylon, chiefly commerce (vv. 3, 7, 9, 11-13, 19). In addition, there is another difference between these two chapters. In chapter 17 it was the beast and his allies who destroyed the harlot Babylon. Here it is God who destroys this aspect of Babylon (v. 8).

ANNOUNCEMENT OF THE JUDGMENT, 18:1-3

The agent of the announcement is another angel who has great power (v. 1). There is no need to refer this to Christ since angels do have great power. In his cry concerning the falling of Babylon he repeats for emphasis "is fallen." He also reveals some facts about Babylon that show how evil the system is and how righteous God is in destroying it.

Babylon is demonic (v. 2). This is emphasized in three phrases. It is the habitation of demons, the hold (prison) of every foul spirit (cf. Eph. 2:2; I John 4:6, where demons are called spirits) and cage ("prison," same word) of every unclean and hateful bird. This latter phrase probably alludes to the birds in the parable of the mustard seed (Matt. 13:31-32) indicating the demonic forces at work in the apostate system.

105

Babylon is unfaithful. This charge of fornication or unfaithfulness to the Lord is repeated in this chapter as in chapter 17.
Babylon is intoxicating. All nations drink of the wine of her unfaithfulness, and merchants particularly have succumbed to her delicacies (literally, luxury or careless ease) and become satisfied with their ill-gained riches. The system pays off her votaries with ease, and they are satisfied. No wonder they weep over her destruction.

APPEAL IN VIEW OF THE JUDGMENT, 18:4-8

STATEMENT, v. 4

The call is to come out of Babylon and not partake of her sins in order to escape her judgments. In its primary interpretation this appeal will be addressed to those believers who will be living in the tribulation days and who like believers in every age will be tempted to compromise. In its application it is a relevant call to believers in every day to avoid compromise with Satan's world system in its every form—religious and commercial. See Genesis 19:12-14; Numbers 16:23-26; Isaiah 48:20; II Corinthians 6:14-17; I John 2:15-17.

SUBSTANTIATION, vv. 5-8

The appeal for separation is substantiated on the basis of three laws.

Remembrance, v. 5. The first Babel confederacy tried to build a tower to heaven (Gen. 11:4); the last piles up her sins to heaven, and God remembers. Although He acts in such long-suffering that men may think He does not notice what is happening, God remembers; and because of this the judgment of Babylon is inevitable and just.

Retribution, v. 6. In the case of Babylon, retributive judgment is doubled in severity because of the enormity of her sins.

Retaliation, vv. 7-8. In place of the glory and luxury with which she has clothed herself, God retaliates with torment and sorrow. The verb that means "lived deliciously" is the same root as the noun meaning "delicacies" in verse 3. In place of her assumed position as queen with many lovers (no widow) God gives plagues, death, mourning and famine. Her lovers are the kings of the earth (17:2; 18:3), but in reality she is a widow because of forsaking the Lord. There is no reason not to understand her final destruction as coming in one day (v. 8). It happened before with another Babylon (Dan. 5:1, 3-5, 30), and it often occurs with individuals (Luke 12:19-20). The burning, too, is to be understood plainly, and evidently refers to the burning of the city or cities which are the center of Babylon in its several forms (which apparently will include Rome). Christians were once burned because they were condemned for having burned Rome. God will burn that city in His judgment on this day.

ANGUISH BECAUSE OF THE JUDGMENT, 18:9-19

KINGS, VV. 9-10

The first lament is from the kings of the earth. They weep and wail when they see the smoke of the fire. Notice that they stand off trying to avoid doom on themselves, but in reality they only postpone it. Again, the suddenness and swiftness of the judgment is emphasized in the phrase "one hour."

MERCHANTS, VV. 11-17a

The merchants of the earth weep and sorrow, for they see the source of their "careless ease" vanishing before their eyes. This motive for their lamentation is plainly stated in 11*b*. It is not that they care about Babylon, but they do care about their businesses. Their merchandise is varied and includes: costly ornaments (gold, silver, precious stones, pearls, 12*a*) ; costly clothes (fine linen, purple, silk, scarlet, 12*b*) ; costly furnishings (thyine wood—a kind of cypress, vessels of ivory, precious wood, brass, iron and marble, 12*c*) ; costly perfumes (cinnamon, odors, ointments, frankincense, 13*a*) ; foods (wine,

oil, fine flour, wheat, 13*b*) ; conveyances (horses, chariots, 13*c*) ;
and even human chattels (slaves—literally, bodies and souls of
men, 13*d*) . Two features should be noted about this list: first,
most of the items are luxury items, and second, apparently
these merchants will be trafficking in people as well as things.
The depth of their sin is covered with the veneer of their
luxurious living.

But in a certain hour of a certain day this will end, and in
the midst of the destruction the merchants will stand afar off,
weeping and sorrowing. They stand off because of the fear
of her torment (v. 15) , and their lament is centered in the fact
that so great riches are come to nought in so short a time (vv.
17-18) . This will be a stock market crash on a worldwide
scale, and in the face of it the thoughts of unsaved men will
only turn to how their own interests are affected. This is
selfishness and greed in its most naked form. *yes!*

SEA MERCHANTS, vv. 17*b*-19

All those connected with commerce on the seas also lament
over the destruction of Babylon. This includes shipmasters
(owners) , sailors, and all who go or work in ships. Their weeping is for the same reason—their business is suddenly being
destroyed.

ACCLAIM OVER THE JUDGMENT, 18:20-24

The reaction of the world to the destruction of Babylon with
all of its business interests has been clearly set forth. The
world weeps, for material things are the only things worldlings
have. When these are destroyed, all is lost. That attitude
which the believers ought to have toward Babylon has also
been stated in verse 4. They should come out from that system and not partake of its sins. Now the reaction of heaven
to the destruction of Babylon is recorded in verses 20-24. The
kings, merchants and mariners bewail the passing of Babylon;
heaven and its friends rejoice. Verse 20 should read, "ye saints,

and apostles and prophets." It also says literally, "God has judged your judgment on her," that is, God has judged your case against her. Babylon had slain the saints; now God slays Babylon. Here is the final answer to the plea of the martyrs in 6:9-11. Then, as if to reassure the citizens of heaven that the destruction is final, an angel takes a millstone and casts it into the sea to symbolize the sure and complete destruction of Babylon (v. 21).

This act brings forth a dirge concerning the total nature of the judgment on Babylon. No music, no worker, no machinery, no light, no happiness ("voice of bridegroom and bride") shall be found in Babylon anymore. The reason is twofold: Babylon deceived the nations and Babylon killed the saints (vv. 23-24).

> Joyless, dark, and silent, Babylon stands out as a monument to the utmost vengeance of God. Wickedness had sat enthroned in the midst of *that* professedly bearing the Name of Christ; but at last, when she had filled to the full her cup of iniquity, God rises in His fierce anger, His indignation burns, and Babylon falls to rise no more. Her destruction is irremediable. The chapter closes with a reiteration of the bloody character of the system.*

---

*Walter Scott, *Exposition of the Revelation of Jesus Christ* (London: Pickering & Inglis, n.d.), p. 373.

XIX

THE SECOND COMING OF CHRIST
19:1-21

JOY IN HEAVEN, 19:1-10

SONGS OF THE SAINTS, vv. 1-6

Time Sequence. "After these things" evidently refers to the visions of the chapters immediately preceding. In 18:20 the call to rejoice was issued; here is the response to that call.

Group involved. The four alleluias come from "a great voice of much people" (v. 1). This is most likely the "great multitude" of 7:9-12. It does not include the twenty-four elders or the four living ones as they are specifically distinguished in verse 4. There is nothing in the text which forbids the inclusion of angels in the group. The word translated "people" in verse 1 is actually "crowd."

Content. The word "alleluia" occurs only in this chapter in the New Testament. The Old Testament renders it "Praise ye the Lord" and it occurs twenty-four times in Psalms. Thus the content of their praise is a song to the Lord. First the crowd praises the righteousness of His judgments particularly illustrated in the judgment of the harlot Babylon (v. 2). The ground of her judgment was her fornication, and her eternal punishment is assured in the phrase "her smoke rose up for ever and ever" (v. 3). Second, the crowd praises the Lord for the fact that He reigns (v. 6). In the meantime the twenty-

four elders and the four living ones have joined in an alleluia
(v. 4), and a voice from heaven has called for additional praise
(v. 5). The voice from the throne is not named though it
probably belongs to an angel.

MARRIAGE OF THE LAMB, VV. 7-10

Announcement of the marriage, v. 7. The marriage is announced as that of the Lamb. Normally a wedding is announced in the name of the bride but not this one. It is His
marriage, and He, not the bride, will be the center of attrac-
tion.

Array of the bride, vv. 7b-8. The delicate balance between
the sovereignty of God and the responsibility of man is main-
tained in the two phrases "hath made herself ready" and "to
her was granted." The bride's array is fine linen which is explained as "the righteousness of the saints." The form of
the word "righteousness" requires the translation "righteous
deeds." In other words, the wedding garment of the bride will
be made up of the righteous deeds done in life. The bride is
the bride because of the righteousness of Christ; the bride is
clothed for the wedding because of her acts. Righteous acts
flow from a righteous character which is entirely of the grace of
God.

Accompaniment of the marriage, v. 9. The wedding is followed by a supper and a special blessing is pronounced upon
those who are called to the supper. These are the friends of the
Bridegroom, and one immediately recalls John 3:29 where
John the Baptist is called a friend of the Bridegroom. These
guests are not the bride and they are not unsaved people, so
they must be redeemed people who are not members of the
church, the body of Christ. The certainty of this beatitude is
underscored by the phrase "these are the true words of God."

Awe of John, v. 10. John seems to have been overawed by
this revelation of the marriage of the Lamb, and he falls at the
feet of the messenger. But he is restrained by words of the

messenger who tells John that he is not deity but a fellow
servant; therefore, he is not to be worshiped or bowed down to.
While Christians recognize the place of angels in carrying out
the purposes of God, and consequently respect them, this verse
clearly shows the impropriety of kneeling at the feet of an
angel. Worship belongs to God. "The witness of Jesus is the
spirit of prophecy" simply means that the study of prophecy
should witness to Jesus.

JUDGMENT ON EARTH, 19:11-21

ADVENT OF CHRIST, VV. 11-16

His aim, v. 11. Again heaven is opened (6:14) but this time
to permit the Lamb to descend to earth in His second coming.
He is on a white horse, and His name is Faithful and True.
This is particularly appropriate to the action which He is
about to take—judging and making war. His purpose in coming is to put down all rebellion by war and by judgment.

His appearance, vv. 12-13. His eyes were as a flame of fire
(1:14), denoting the penetrating quality of His judgment.
On His head were many crowns, indicating His majesty and
sovereignty. The name which no man knew is just that, un-
revealed. His vesture was a garment dipped in blood, a strik-
ing picture since this is before He enters into battle. It is a
sure token of the righteous vengeance which will shortly be
meted out in that battle. He also carries the name "The Word
of God." This is a title used only by John (John 1:1, 14;
I John 1:1; 5:7).

His army, v. 14. His army is apparently composed of saints
since the clothing is the same as in verse 8.

His authority, vv. 15-16. His authority is seen in the sharp
sword (1:16; 2:12, 16), in his taking up the rule of the nations,
in the figure of treading out the winepress (14:20), and in the
name King of kings and Lord of lords. The word for "rule"
(v. 15) is literally "shepherd." This shepherd will use a rod
of iron on the nations.

ARMAGEDDON CONFLICT, VV. 17-21

Carnage, vv. 17-18. So great will be the slaughter in the war of Armageddon that an angel calls together the fowls of heaven to eat the flesh of those who fall in the battle. The victims will include kings, captains, mighty men, horses, riders, bondmen and freemen. The phrase at the end of verse 17 literally reads "the great supper of God." What an ignoble end for these many nobles and others.

Conflict, v. 19. The beast and his followers and other leaders and their followers gather together to make war with the Lamb. The world resists God to the bitter end.

Captives, v. 20. The two leaders, the beast and the false prophet—the two characters of chapter 13—are taken captive alive and cast into the lake of fire and brimstone. They are still there one thousand years later (20:10) and will be forever.

Conquest, v. 21. The remnant (that is, the rest) were killed by the Lord. Deprived of their leaders, the rest of the people are quickly conquered. His victory will be complete.

XX

THE MILLENNIUM AND THE
GREAT WHITE THRONE
20:1-15

CHAPTER 20 is like the calm after the storm. In the major outline of the book, this chapter is the second part of the third
main section of the book. The third section includes the things
which shall be hereafter (chaps. 4—22). The first part of this
section was the description of the tribulation period (chaps.
4—19) ; this second part is the millennium (chap. 20) and the
third part will be the eternal state (chaps. 21—22).

THE MILLENNIUM, 20:1-10
SATAN, VV. 1-3

During the millennial age Satan will be bound and out of
action until the very end. The agent that binds Satan is an
angel. He is an angel to whom this authority has been given
because he has the key to the bottomless pit and a chain (cf.
II Peter 2:4 and Jude 6 where chains are used to confine spirit
beings). The duration of his confinement will be a thousand
years. This is to be understood as literally as other figures in
the book. The purpose of his being bound is "that he should
deceive the nations no more" (v. 3). However, at the end of
that period he will be loosed "a little season."

114

SAINTS, VV. 4-6

John apparently saw three groups of saints in verse 4. He saw first those who sat on the thrones and who shared in the judging, apparently a reference to the church (cf. I Cor. 6:2; II Tim. 2:12). Then he saw a particular group of martyrs— those who were beheaded. Literally the word means killed with an ax. This means of execution was practiced in ancient Rome. Finally, he saw those who had refused to worship the beast and receive his mark. They (referring to this last group) live and reign with Christ for this millennial period. The others will have already been raised at the rapture, but this last group will be raised at the second coming of Christ.

The rest of the dead, that is the unsaved dead, are not raised at this time according to verse 5. They will be raised after the one thousand years. Therefore there is not one general resurrection. The first resurrection includes all those who believe, since those included in the first resurrection are called blessed (v. 6). Over them the second death (cf. v. 14) has no power as it does over the unsaved dead. The Lord indicated this same distinction of two resurrections in John 5:29, but did not specify the time difference between the two.

SINNERS, VV. 7-10

As predicted in verse 3, Satan will be loosed at the close of the thousand-year reign of Christ on the earth. He will find plenty of people who will follow his deception, their number being as the sand of the sea. Gog and Magog in verse 8 remind one of Ezekiel 38—39 but this is obviously not the same battle since the time is different (Ezek. 38:16) and the judgment is dissimilar (Ezek. 38:19-22). The host of followers of Satan will besiege the camp of God in Jerusalem and will be put to death quickly by an act of God sending fire down out of heaven to devour them. Then the devil is cast into the lake of fire where the beast and false prophet have already been for one thousand years.

Where will this large number of followers of Satan come from? When the millennium begins, people with earthly bodies will enter it, but apparently none of them will be unsaved at the beginning. But very soon (perhaps in the first minutes) babies will be born and in one thousand years many children will be born, grow up and live unusually long lives. All of them will be obliged to give outward allegiance to Christ who reigns on the throne, but as in every age He will not compel them to believe with their hearts. Consequently there will be many living who have never turned to Christ for salvation, though they have obeyed Him as Head of the government. These will seize on the chance to give expression of the rebellion of their hearts when Satan arises to be their leader in this last revolt. The millennium will prove, among other things, that a perfect earthly environment and even universal knowledge of the Lord will not change men's hearts. This must be done personally, and multitudes will never have experienced it during that long period.

GREAT WHITE THRONE JUDGMENT, 20:11-15

TIME

This judgment follows the close of the millennium.

JUDGE

The Judge is One from whose face the earth and the heaven flee away. According to John 5:22 the Father has given all judgment into the hands of the Son; therefore, the Judge must be Christ. The words "before God" in verse 12 should read "before the throne" and thus constitute no contradiction.

SUBJECTS

Those who stand in this judgment are the dead, small and great. Christians are described as the "dead in Christ" (I Thess. 4:16). These are the unsaved dead of all ages. This includes dead in the sea and the dead whose bodies have been claimed by death and whose souls have been claimed by Hades (v. 13). They all stand before Christ on this occasion.

BASIS

The basis for judgment is expressly said to be the works of these people (vv. 12-13). These are apparently contained in the books mentioned in verse 12, and the book of life is opened only to show that no name of anyone standing before the throne is written in it. Rejection of the Saviour places men in this judgment (and excludes their names from the book of life), but works done in life prove that they deserve eternal punishment. It is almost like a final act of grace for Christ to show men that on the basis of their own records they deserve the lake of fire.

RESULT

The result of this judgment is that all of those who are in it are cast into the lake of fire. This is the second death—eternal separation from God. Even death (which claims the body) and Hades (which claims the soul) are cast into the lake of fire since their work is now done. The death men die on earth is only temporary. All will partake of resurrection. The prison of the soul at death, Hades, is also temporary; for the final separation, the second death, is in the lake of fire.

XXI

THE ETERNAL STATE

21:1—22:5

To REVIEW, the major outline of the book is taken from 1:19. The third section, "the things which shall be hereafter," comprises chapters 4—22. That section is divided chronologically into three parts: the tribulation (chaps. 4—19), the millennium (chap. 20) and the eternal state (21:1—22:5).

Throughout these last two chapters of Revelation the discussion concerns a city, the new Jerusalem. That this is the description of eternity seems apparent from the phrases in 21:1 and the close association between verses 1 and 2. Almost all commentators recognize this. Some, however, feel that 21:9-21 reverts to a description of the millennial state. This would seem incongruent with the chronological pattern of the book and of this section. Perhaps the best way to understand this entire section is to regard the new Jerusalem as the abode of the redeemed of all ages. Conditions within the new Jerusalem are conditions of eternity. Of course the redeemed will be inhabiting the city during the millennium as well as during eternity. Always the conditions within the city are eternal, even when the city is related to the millennium. This is no different from the present, for loved ones in heaven are enjoying eternal conditions as is God even though these eternal conditions impinge on time (as, for instance, on the Mount of Transfiguration or this entire vision given to John in the revelation). In other words, the new Jerusalem is the abode of the redeemed during the millennium and during eternity.

DESCENT OF THE CITY, 21:1-8

Three phrases in verse 1 underscore the fact that eternity is now being described. (1) This is a new heaven and new earth. The word for "new" means new in quality—"it suggests fresh life rising from the decay and wreck of the old world."* Both heaven and earth are included in this new creation. (2) The old had passed away. (3) There was no more sea. Whatever else this phrase may mean, it seems to indicate the end of the old order (Exodus 20:11; Ezek. 48:28). As understood literally this indicates a complete change in climatic conditions.

John then saw the new Jerusalem. The writer to the Hebrews speaks of this heavenly Jerusalem as the abode of the saints (Heb. 12:22-24). John identifies it as the bride. The city comes down out of heaven to be related to the earth in some way, but this does not mean that conditions within the city are earthly. Indeed, verses 3-8 are a detailed explanation of the newness of the city.

The first characteristic of the new condition is God with men, v. 3. God Himself will dwell with men during eternity.

Old experiences will be excluded, vv. 4-5. God will wipe away every tear (the Greek is singular). Death will vanish and with it sorrow, crying and pain. These negatives are summarized in a positive statement in verse 5: "Behold, I make all things new." Then John is instructed by God who sits on the throne to write, for the words are true. Probably John was so overwhelmed at what he was seeing and learning that he forgot momentarily to write (cf. 14:13; 19:9).

New things will be experienced, vv. 6-7. First, a complete satisfaction ("the fountain of the water of life"); second, a full inheritance (v. 7a), and third, full fellowship (v. 7b).

*Henry Barclay Swete, *The Apocalypse of St. John* (London: Macmillan, 1907), p. 275.

Certain people are excluded, v. 8. People who are characterized by any of these eight traits listed here will be in the lake
of fire and, thus, excluded from heaven. Notice that the text
does not say that anyone who has ever committed any of these
sins will be excluded, but people whose lives are characterized
in these ways. There is a difference, for instance, in ever telling a lie and being a liar as the habit of one's life.

Description of the City, 21:9-27

John is now bidden by one of the angels who poured out the
bowl judgments to view the city in greater detail. Again the
city is identified as the bride of Christ (v. 9). This is the place
which Christ has gone to prepare for His people (John 14:2).
This section describes the city's relation to the millennial
state. In other words, there seem to be two descents of the city,
21:1-8 being the one in relation to eternity and 21:9—22:5 the
one in relation to the millennium.

glory, v. 11

The glory of the city is the glory of God. Her light is the
radiance of God's complete character, light as a valuable gem,
clear as crystal reflecting the fullness of the facets of God's
person.

construction, vv. 12-14

The city had a great and high wall, suggesting the security
of the bride. In the wall are twelve gates with an angel at
each one and the names of the twelve tribes of Israel inscribed
on them. There are three gates on each of the four sides. The
wall has twelve foundations and on them are the names of the
twelve apostles. Notice that even in eternity Israel and the
church are distinguished, though both are included in God's
redeemed people.

MEASUREMENTS, VV. 15-17

The angel that talked with John had a golden reed (ten feet long) to measure the city, gates and wall. Nothing further is said about the gates, but the city measures 12,000 furlongs or 1,500 miles and it is in the shape of a cube, foursquare. This is about the distance from the Pacific coast of the United States to the Mississippi River. The cube or foursquare shape of the city reminds one of the fourfold dimensions given of the love of God (Eph. 3:18). The wall measures 144 cubits or 216 feet high, and these measurements by the angel are the same as human measurements. No different figures are to be imagined. Concerning the foursquare shape of the city, Swete has a worthwhile comment.

> The tetragon occurs more than once in the legislation of Exodus. Both the altar of burnt offering and the altar of incense were of this form (Ex. xxvii.1, xxx.2), and so was the High Priest's breastplate (*ib.*xxviii.16, xxxvi.16–xxxix.9); the feature reappears in Ezekiel's new city and temple (Ez. xli.21, xliii.16, xlv.1, xlviii.20). In Solomon's Temple the Holy of Holies was a perfect cube, 20 cubits each way. . . . In ancient cities the foursquare form was not unusual. . . . As is well known, the rectangular tetragon was to Greek thinkers a symbol of perfection.†

MATERIALS, VV. 18-21

The wall was of jasper (usually green quartz) and the city of pure gold—both clear as crystal. The foundation was adorned (a word from which we derive the English word "cosmetics") with precious stones. The colors are as follows: jasper, green; sapphire, blue; chalcedony, green; emerald, green; sardonyx, brown and white; sardius, red; chrysolyte, yellow; beryl, green; topaz, yellow; chrysoprasus, apple green; jacinth, blue; amethyst, purple. The gates were pearls and the street (not

†Swete, *Op. cit.*, p. 284.

streets) was pure, transparent gold. Our earthly minds trying to comprehend heaven certainly understand from this description that it is a place of extreme beauty.

RELATION TO GOD, vv. 22-23

The city does not require a temple or a place of worship and access to God simply because God and the Lamb are actually present and themselves constitute the temple. The city requires no sun or moon since the glory of God and the Lamb will light the city. This does not mean that there will be no sun or moon, but only that they will not be required for light within the city.

RELATION TO NATIONS, vv. 24-27

Nations and kings on the earth will bring glory and honor to the city. Many feel that the mention of nations here shows that the time referred to is the millennium and we are viewing the relation of the new Jerusalem which is suspended over the earth during the millennium to the people on the earth. However, entrance into the city is restricted to those who are redeemed (v. 27).

DELIGHTS OF THE CITY, 22:1-5

FULLNESS OF LIFE AND BLESSING, vv. 1-2

The source of the river is the throne of God and the Lamb and, like the city, it is clear as crystal. The river is the water of life, and its presence in the city simply means that fullness of life will be the experience of all those who inhabit it. The tree of life (cf. Gen. 2:9; Rev. 2:7), is also an assurance of fullness of life in that city. The tree yields fruit constantly, indicating the continuous blessing that will pour forth. Its leaves are for the healing of the nations, which again indicates blessing of some sort.

FULLNESS OF PARADISE, VV. 3-5

Paradise excludes the curse (v. 3) and all darkness (v. 5). Paradise includes the privilege of serving God and the Lamb (v. 3), of seeing His face, and of having His name on our foreheads—a proof of complete consecration to God's service. The word for service is *latreuo,* a priestly service. Paradise is not only the absence of evil but the privilege of serving God in His presence forever. It also means reigning with Him forever and ever. This is complete exaltation and perfect exultation.

XXII

EPILOGUE

22:6-21

THE EPILOGUE to the book comprises most of chapter 22 (vv. 6-21). It consists of words of comfort and words of caution.

WORDS OF COMFORT, 22:6-17

"THESE SAYINGS ARE FAITHFUL AND TRUE," v. 6

Elsewhere in the book there have been solemn affirmations of the veracity of the prophecies (15:3; 16:7; 19:2). The remainder of verse 6 is like 1:1.

"I COME QUICKLY," v. 7

This reminder of the imminency of the Lord's coming is accompanied by a promise of blessing for those who keep the sayings of the book. This, too, is like the opening (1:3).

GOD IS WORTHY OF WORSHIP, vv. 8-9

Again John, overawed, bows down at the feet of the revealing angel to worship him (as in 19:10). Again he is reprimanded and reminded that God is the One to be worshiped. The angel takes his place with the fellow servants and prophets as a creature of God and therefore unworthy of worship.

THE BOOK IS NOT SEALED, VV. 10-11

The book is not to be sealed since the time is near and people will need to understand what God is doing (cf. Dan. 12:4). When the time is fulfilled, that is, when Christ comes, then destinies will be fixed. This is the meaning of verse 11. The unjust and filthy will remain this way forever, as will the righteous and holy.

REWARDS WILL BE GIVEN, VV. 12-13

Verse 12 includes the second occurrence of the words "behold I come quickly." But this time the assurance of the giving of rewards is added. Salvation is entirely of grace, but rewards are based on works (I Cor. 3:11-15). This is certified by the One who is Alpha and Omega (cf. 1:8, 11, 17; 2:8).

BLESSED ARE THE REDEEMED, VV. 14-15

"Blessed" is used seven times in the book, this being the last (cf. 1:3; 14:13; 16:15; 19:9; 20:6; 22:7). The better reading instead of "do his commandments" is "wash their robes." Blessed are the redeemed who will have the right to the tree of life (eternal life) and entrance into the joys of the new Jerusalem. Those who have not washed their robes in the blood of the Lamb are described as "without" or "outside."

GRACIOUS IS OUR LORD, VV. 16-17

He is gracious because He is the One who sent His angel to reveal these things to John and the churches. How enlarged is our understanding and how different our perspective simply because the Lord chose to reveal these things about the future. He is gracious because He is the root of David and thus the basis for the fulfillment of all of Israel's covenanted promises. He is gracious because He is the bright and morning star assuring that a new day will dawn. He is gracious because He still offers grace to anyone who will come to drink of the water

of life freely (v. 17) . The Spirit and the bride join in this call
to the unsaved.

WORDS OF WARNING, 22:18-19

ADDING TO THE BOOK, v. 18

If anyone adds to the words of the prophecy, God will add to
him the many and varied plagues written in it (cf. Deut. 4:2;
Prov. 30:6) .

SUBTRACTING FROM THE BOOK, v. 19

Subtraction means exclusion from the book of life, the holy
city, and the promises and blessings of this prophecy. This
can mean only the lake of fire, for all who are not written in
the book of life are cast into that place. These are solemn
warnings against tampering in any way with the prophecies
of this book of Revelation.

CLOSING BENEDICTION, 22:20-21

For the third time in this chapter (vv. 7, 12) the Lord says
that He will come quickly. John's reply is, "Come, Lord Jesus."
John concludes with the customary benediction, "The grace
of our Lord Jesus Christ be with you all. Amen."

SOME HELPFUL COMMENTARIES
ON REVELATION

CRISWELL, W. A. *Expository Sermons on Revelation*. Grand Rapids: Zondervan Publishing House, 1962-66, 5 vols. These are not only excellent expository sermons but they contain careful exegesis. The viewpoint is premillennial and pretribulational.

NEWELL, WILLIAM R. *The Book of the Revelation*. Chicago: Moody Press, 1935. Consistently literal in interpretation. Very helpful appendixes.

SCOTT, WALTER. *Exposition of the Revelation of Jesus Christ*. London: Pickering & Inglis, n.d. This is the fountainhead of all the subsequent "Plymouth Brethren" commentaries. It is very thorough and helpful.

SEISS, J. A. *The Apocalypse*. Grand Rapids: Zondervan Publishing House, 1865. This older commentary is still very helpful.

SMITH, J. B. *A Revelation of Jesus Christ*. Scottdale, Pa.: Herald Press, 1961. The author, a Mennonite, has written a detailed exegesis of Revelation from the pretribulational, premillennial viewpoint. There are many statistics and comparisons included.

STRAUSS, LEHMAN. *The Book of the Revelation*. Neptune, N. J.: Loizeaux Brothers, 1964. An excellent, popular work.

SWETE, HENRY BARCLAY. *The Apocalypse of St. John*. London: Macmillan, 1907. Helpful for Greek exegesis but not futuristic in viewpoint.

WALVOORD, JOHN F. *The Revelation of Jesus Christ*. Chicago: Moody Press, 1966. Careful and detailed exegesis from the pretribulation, premillennial viewpoint.